Making Sense of Micronesia

Making Sense
OF MICRONESIA

《 • 《 • 《 • 《 • 《 • 《 • 《 • 《 • 《 • 》 • 》 • 》 • 》 • 》 • 》 • 》 • 》 • 》

The Logic of Pacific Island Culture

FRANCIS X. HEZEL, S.J.

University of Hawai'i Press
HONOLULU

Library of Congress Cataloging-in-Publication Data

Hezel, Francis X.
Making sense of Micronesia : the logic of Pacific island culture /
Francis X. Hezel, SJ.
    pages cm
    Includes bibliographical references and index.
    ISBN 978-0-8248-3661-0 (cloth : alk. paper)
    1. Micronesia—Social life and customs. 2. Micronesia—
Civilization. I. Title.
    DU500.H48 2013
    996.5—dc23
                                                    2012028879

Maps by Manoa Mapworks, Inc. Courtesy of Center
for Pacific Islands Studies, University of Hawai'i at Mānoa

Designed by Josie Herr

Printed by Sheridan Books, Inc.

Contents

PREFACE

This short book is written for those interested in but unfamiliar with Micronesian island societies and how they work. At one time that would have meant expatriate teachers, physicians, and lawyers who have contracted to work in the islands, as well as volunteers and church personnel assigned there. Today, when tens of thousands of Micronesians have emigrated to the United States, the audience may be larger. It might include the American teachers, health providers, social workers, and others who find themselves puzzled by the island people who make up part of their clientele. Where once westerners had to visit the western Pacific to encounter these islanders and their ways, now the cultural exchanges are taking place on American turf in hundreds of communities, large and small.

The purpose of this book is to lay out some of the basic principles in Micronesian culture, at least as I have come to understand it. By this I don't mean the exotic externals of the culture—the outward trappings of island culture that so often capture the attention of outsiders. This book is not about oceangoing canoes or navigational techniques; it's not about island dances or feasts, lavalavas or loincloths, or curious ceremonies related to birth or death. It is about the pattern of values and attitudes that underlie the externals of island culture—a pattern that makes good sense, providing we focus on island realities and needs. Culture is not just a willy-nilly collection of quaint practices, although it may often appear that way to outsiders. There is a logic to island culture and that logic is what I wish to represent here.

In the course of mapping the basic features of this pattern, or logic, I'll be highlighting some of the points of conflict between traditional island culture and the demands of the modern world. We might call these points of conflict the "dilemmas of development." In many cases, as I will try to show, the very features of island culture that were highly functional in the past, some of them remaining so even today, seem to inhibit what we now consider "development." Changes may have to be made, as they must in any culture, but we outsiders should at least understand some of the broader context of island culture before we begin leading the charge for social change according to our own formulas.

My hope is that in this book I might be able to pass on a bit of what I've learned over the course of some forty years to others who are trying to make some sense of Micronesian ways. I approach this task as a lifelong learner, one who first stumbled upon the islands in 1963 when, as a young Jesuit, I was assigned to teach at Xavier High School in Chuuk. I may have begun my work back then with a grand sense of what I hoped to accomplish, but it didn't take me long to appreciate the depth of my ignorance about the people for whom I was working. There followed a long schooling in the culture and ways of the islands—a happy but humbling experience that continues even up to the present. What I have to share in this book, then, is what I've managed to pick up over the course of my long journey.

This book has many limitations. It makes no claim to being academic and is without the scholarly notes and bibliography that usually confer authority on a published work. The sources are my own experiences in the islands and what I have managed to digest from the experiences of others, whether published or not. The composite view of the culture presented here, although it owes more than I can acknowledge to the work of others, is always filtered through my own experience in the islands. Generalizations abound, simply asserted, with the finer distinctions ignored. The cultural distinctiveness of the many different island groups is deliberately blurred so as to retain focus on general cultural patterns throughout the area. The result is something of a cultural puree, a blend of the several cultures within the area. Likewise, the distinction between past and present has been largely glossed over here so that island cultures seem to be frozen in their "traditional" state. (Anyone who wishes a more detailed review of the cultural change that has occurred in the last three generations may consult my previous book, *The New Shape of Old Island Cultures*.) Finally, the gap between western values and practice and those in Micronesia is exaggerated at times precisely in order to highlight the contrast. Because nuances are lost in a book like this, island ways and western ways may both seem like caricatures.

Micronesians who want to peek over the shoulders of the uninitiated to read these pages should be warned that they might not like what they see, for those reasons just listed and for others besides. Islanders seem to cherish the sense of mystery that surrounds their culture and makes it impenetrable to western eyes. At bottom, no one wants to see the guts of one's culture laid out on the table for all to see, especially when some of the vital organs may appear to have been lost or mislabeled. With this I can express sympathy but not full agreement. Oversimplification is the price we almost always pay for analysis. But let me presume to suggest that even for Micronesians there may be something to be learned here, just as Americans have taken away food for thought from the books that were written about their own culture.

When the word "islands" is used in this book, it is intended to refer to that area that many of us call Micronesia. That would include the broad cultural expanse in the western Pacific north of the equator, comprising everything from Palau to the Marshall Islands, including the four states and five distinct culture-language areas found in what is now the Federated States of Micronesia. In a broader sense, of course, the term might apply also to Guam and the Northern Mariana Islands, although these places have become far more acculturated. Much of what is written here might even apply to other island groups throughout the Pacific. Without making any claims in that regard, let me suggest, as my father once would have put it, that "if the shoe fits, wear it."

Let me conclude by begging the indulgence of my Micronesian friends, who have taught me all this and much more, for the liberties I've taken in presenting their island cultures this way. I offer my apologies if what I have written here seems patronizing in any way. My hope is that it may save the uninitiated a little of the effort that so many of us have had to go through to piece together a basic cultural map of the island societies that we have come to love.

Acknowledgments

It is impossible to name here the hundreds of Micronesians who have patiently borne my blunders as they taught me bit by bit to view life through their eyes. To them I dedicate this book, but with the warning that they may have to exercise their patience yet again if they read it.

At the risk of offending unnamed others, let me mention here a few who have especially contributed. Euke Samuel, Vita Skilling, Angie Van Horn, and their families along with the people of Wonei and Paata who steered me through my early introduction to Chuukese culture deserve mention. Bishop Amando and his Micronesian diocesan priests have provided support and guidance throughout the years. On Pohnpei I had the privilege of living for a time with the families of Adalino Lorens and Kasi Kilmete, while others like Gus Kohler, Rufino Mauricio, and Canis Cantero repeatedly offered assistance as I tried to make sense of the culture. Bryan and Tasia Isaac welcomed me into their home time and again, as did Marcus and Maggie Samo. To all of them, and to so many others not named here, I am grateful.

My older brother Jesuits—Bill McGarry, Jack Curran, Joe Cavanagh, and Dick Hoar, among others—have provided critical insights, a stockpile of stories, and strong encouragement when I faltered. Two deceased Micronesian Jesuits, Felix Yaoch and Apollo Thall, gave generously of their wisdom and provided a broad cultural bridge for me as for so many others.

The community of anthropologists and others who have studied and written on the islands kindly offered me the fruits of their own labor. Bob Kiste, Mac Marshall, Glenn Petersen, Ken Rehg, David Hanlon, and Jay Dobbin instantly come to mind, but there are so many more.

Finally, I'd like to pay tribute to Elsa Veloso and Jason Aubuchon, as well as others on the Micronesian Seminar staff—including Sapna Urhekar, Liza Austria, and Erik Steffen—for their support in more ways than I can recall.

To all of them and the many others who made this work possible, my profound thanks. I hope that I get at least some of it right here. If not, I accept the blame.

Introduction

Micronesia—"the tiny islands," as they were labeled by a nineteenth-century French naval captain—live up to their name. A couple of the largest are about one hundred square miles, but most are far smaller, the smallest with a land area of no more than a few acres. There are close to two thousand of them in all, but only about one hundred are inhabited. They include mountainous volcanic islands, slabs of continental shelf, and coral atolls that rise only a few feet above sea level.

The islands stretch in a long arc more than two thousand miles across the northwestern Pacific close to the equator. The term "Micronesia," as we will use it here, includes Palau in the extreme west, the Marshall Islands at the eastern end, and everything in between—that is to say, what is now called the Federated States of Micronesia, which includes the four states of Yap, Chuuk, Pohnpei, and Kosrae. There are other island groups that might be called part of Micronesia in the broad sense of the term—Guam and the Mariana Islands, Kiribati and Nauru—but we will not be discussing them in this book. Let me note, however, that much of what is written here would probably also apply to these groups.

The History

Micronesia was first settled a century or two before the Christian Era by seafarers who had worked their way from Taiwan down the islands off East Asia and moved into the Melanesian islands to the south. Even before they sailed north to occupy the uninhabited islands of

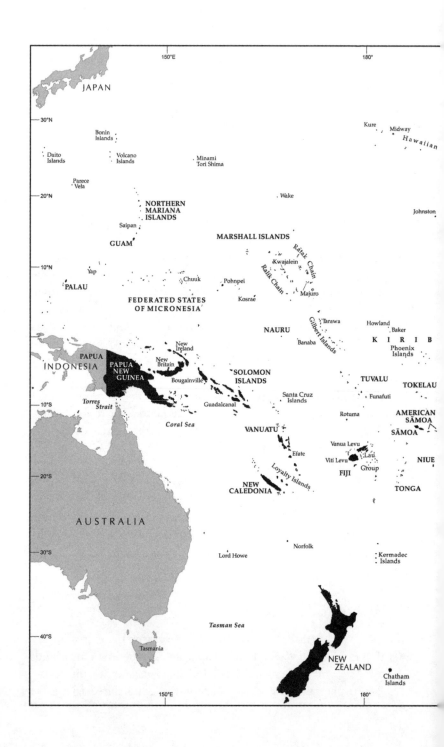

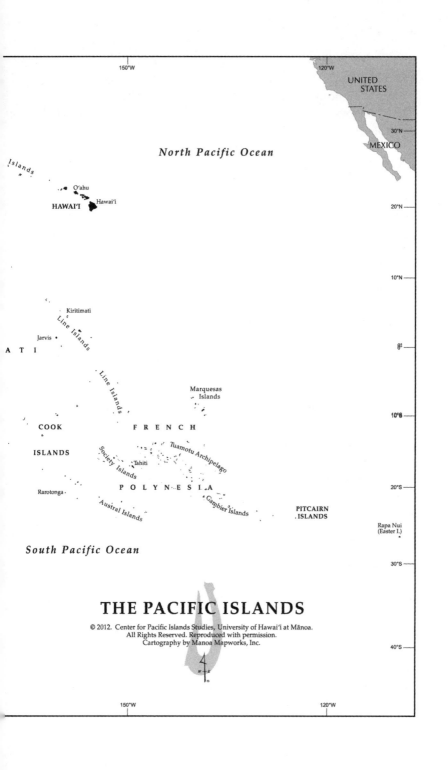

Islands

North Pacific Ocean

UNITED
STATES

MEXICO

30°N

O'ahu
HAWAI'I   Hawai'i

20°N

10°N

Kiritimati

Line Islands

Jarvis

A T I

0°

Line Islands

Marquesas
Islands

10°S

COOK

F R E N C H

ISLANDS

Tuamotu Archipelago

Society Islands

Tahiti

P O L Y N E S I A

20°S

Rarotonga

Gambier Islands

PITCAIRN
ISLANDS

Austral Islands

Rapa Nui
(Easter I.)

30°S

South Pacific Ocean

40°S

THE PACIFIC ISLANDS

150°W

120°W

150°W

120°W

eastern and central Micronesia, others from offshore Asia settled in Palau and Yap.

It wasn't until the 1500s, when Spanish ships began crossing the Pacific in search of the highly prized goods from the "Spice Islands" and the Orient, that the islands of Micronesia began appearing on western maps. The sporadic visits to these islands during the Age of Discovery were followed by a two-hundred-year lull in European voyages to the Pacific, while Europeans attended to their own wars. In the 1800s contact between the West and Micronesian islanders resumed, as China traders and whaleships crisscrossed the Pacific on commercial voyages and European and American naval expeditions set about mapping the region.

In the early 1850s the first missionaries, American Protestants, arrived in the islands. They were followed thirty years later by Catholic missionaries. By the end of the century Christianity was well established throughout island Micronesia. So was the copra trade, which allowed islanders to acquire basic western goods such as iron cooking utensils, steel tools, cloth and clothing, guns, and select imported foods. During the century Micronesians had adopted a western religion, hosted a number of resident beachcombers and traders, learned a smattering of English, acquired some foreign goods, and picked up some familiarity with western ways. Still, their basic island cultural system remained intact.

A century of colonial rule over the islands began in 1885 when Spain laid claim to the Caroline Islands and Germany annexed the Marshall Islands. It was the age of colonization when western powers were carving up the developing world and seizing colonies as status symbols if not for their raw materials. The United States acquired its own first colonies at about this time: Guam, Puerto Rico, the Philippines, and American Samoa. In 1899, following the Spanish-American War, Germany took over Spain's holdings in the Carolines and so laid claim to just about all of Micronesia.

At the outbreak of World War I in 1914, Japan seized the islands from Germany and later legitimized its rule when Micronesia was recognized as a League of Nations mandate at the end of the war. Japan established the first public education system in the islands. It also undertook large-scale development projects that included phosphate mining, sugar cultivation, fishing, and pearling. To provide the labor

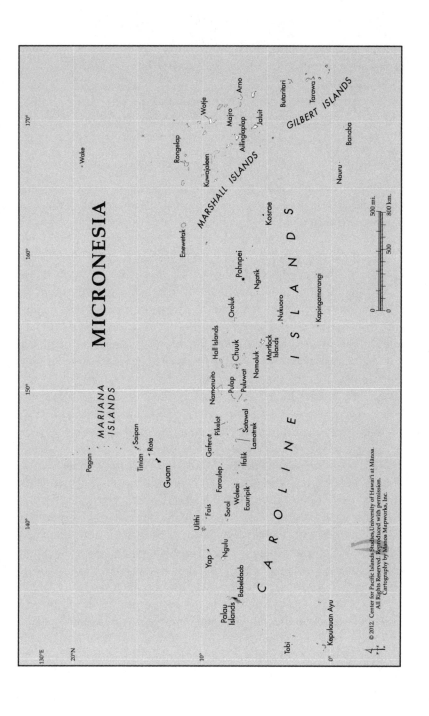

MICRONESIA

130°E

20°N

Wake

MARIANA ISLANDS

Pagan

Tinian Saipan
       Rota

Guam

Rongelap

Enewetok

Kuwajalein

MARSHALL ISLANDS

Kosrae

Pohnpei

Ngatik

Oroluk

Nukuoro

Mortlock Islands

Namoluk

Chuuk

Puluwat

Pulap

Hall Islands

Namonuito

Satawal

Lamotrek

Ifalik

Pikelot

Gaferut

Ulithi

Fais

Farulep

Sorol

Woleai

Eauripik

Yap

Ngulu

Palau Islands

Babeldaob

CAROLINE

ISLANDS

Kapingamarangi

10°

Majro

Aur

Wotje

Arno

Ailinglaplap

Jaluit

GILBERT ISLANDS

Butaritari

Tarawa

Nauru

Banaba

160°

170°

150°

140°

Tobi

Kepulauan Ayu

0°

© 2012 Center for Pacific Islands Studies, University of Hawai'i at Mānoa.
All Rights Reserved. Reproduced with permission.
Cartography by Mānoa Mapworks, Inc.

0   500   500 mi.
0   500   800 km.

needed for all this, Japan brought in so many of its own citizens that Japanese outnumbered islanders in Micronesia even before the start of World War II.

The islands were surrendered by Japan to the United States at the end of the war. (For the third time colonial rule had passed from one power to another as a result of a war.) Just as Japan had exercised authority over the islands with the blessings of the League of Nations, the United States now administered the islands as a trust territory of the United Nations. Soon the trappings of western democracy were introduced to the islands: popular elections, the chartering of municipalities, and the councils that would later become legislative bodies in each island group. But the infrastructure that the Japanese had built up before the war was not restored, so the island economy remained a shadow of what it had been during the height of Japanese productivity.

During the 1960s, the United States stepped up its budget and its expectations of its island ward. As the trust territory's subsidy grew each year, education and health services were expanded and thousands more islanders were added to the government payroll. The first local law-making body was set up for the territory, and plans were laid for determining a future political status for the islands. Meanwhile, the size of towns grew as hundreds moved in to seek cash employment. Soon Micronesia had the groundwork for a dual economy: a cash economy in some of the towns superimposed on a traditional subsistence economy in more rural areas.

Micronesians initiated political status negotiations with the United States and convoked a constitutional convention in 1975. Three years later the United States granted the islands self-rule. By that time the former trust territory was forever dissolved, for the islands had split into several political units. While the Northern Mariana Islands remained attached to the United States as a commonwealth, the remainder of the trust territory broke up into the Federated States of Micronesia (FSM), the Republic of Palau, and the Republic of the Marshall Islands. Although the three governments began to function by 1979, several years passed before the three nations were recognized as independent and became full members of the United Nations. Official recognition came in 1986 for FSM and the Marshalls, and in 1992 for Palau.

The three island nations, although now independent, are bound to the United States by a Compact of Free Association. This compact grants the United States certain military and defense rights, while providing yearly financial assistance to the island nations. Even so, the economy in these countries has been largely stagnant since independence. A great number of islanders have been emigrating to the United States in search of the jobs they cannot find on their own islands.

The Islands

Marshalls (population 53,000). This easternmost part of Micronesia is composed of two chains of coral atolls running north and south. Crops and plant life are fewer and rainfall lighter on these coral atolls than in other parts of Micronesia. In the past pandanus was one of the chief staple foods. Despite its limited resources, the Marshalls had a Polynesian-like authority system headed by paramount chiefs, or *irooj,* that distinguished it from other coral atolls in the region. Chiefly authority in the Marshalls even today remains stronger than in any other part of Micronesia. Marshallese, like many other Micronesian peoples, derive their membership in a clan and lineage from their mother. At one time people may have tended to live in lineage groups on parcels of land inherited from their mothers, but residence groups are now more mixed.

The Marshalls is an independent nation today. Its capital is located in Majuro, an atoll that contains over half of the population of the country. Kwajalein, the other heavily populated atoll, is the site of a U.S. missile range that has been in operation for over fifty years. Hundreds of Marshallese living on nearby islands in the atoll hold jobs on the Kwajalein base.

Kosrae (population 6,600). Kosrae, now a state in FSM, is a single high island with a cultural tradition that was once very similar to Pohnpei's. During the nineteenth century, however, Kosrae suffered a drastic loss of population brought on by western diseases that left the island with only three hundred people by the end of the century. As a consequence, many of the traditional institutions collapsed. They were replaced by social and political structures introduced by the American Protestant missionaries then working on the island. All but a few of the people in Kosrae today are members of the Protestant Church. Rank and prestige are acquired through church office or a high position in the government. Married couples usually live on the husband's land as part of a larger kin group. Many Kosraeans still support themselves by cultivating breadfruit and taro and by fishing, but the island has lost nearly two thousand people in the last ten years due to emigration.

Pohnpei (population 36,000). Pohnpei is the capital of the Federated States of Micronesia. The high island of Pohnpei, with an area of about one hundred square miles, is one of the largest in Micronesia. In addition, the state includes seven coral atolls, some with different languages. In contrast with Chuuk and the coral atolls in central Micronesia, Pohnpei has always had a strongly developed chiefly system. There are five chiefdoms on the main island, each headed by its own high chief (*Nahnmwarki*) and under-chief (*Nahniken*). Offerings of traditional prestige foods at feasts and funerals—pigs, yams, and kava (called *sakau*)—have always been a major feature of the culture. Although the society is organized into matrilineages, children inherit their land from their father and married couples usually reside on the husband's family estate. Pohnpeians in rural areas generally live in homesteads scattered over the countryside rather than in the more compact villages that are found in other parts of Micronesia.

Chuuk (population 49,000). The heart of this state in FSM is a barrier reef embracing a number of rather small volcanic islands. This center, Chuuk Lagoon, is surrounded by several coral atolls to the north, west, and south, a few of which have retained even to the present their traditional dress of loincloths and lavalavas. Authority was so fragmented that individual islands were seldom unified under a single chief, and this island group still remains much more politically fragmented than other parts of Micronesia. This has hampered the development of the state, with the result that the education system and infrastructure lag behind most other island groups in Micronesia. In recent years thousands of Chuukese have emigrated to the United States to seek employment and good education.

The main social unit has always been the lineage group, descended from a single living woman. The staple crops in Chuuk are breadfruit and taro. In contrast to most other parts of Micronesia, women in Chuuk do offshore fishing while men work in the taro patches and pick breadfruit.

Yap (population 11,000). This westernmost state in the FSM is divided into two different cultural and language groups: a cluster of high islands with its own distinct language, and a chain of coral atolls in which people speak a language closely related to Chuukese. This state has the reputation of being the most traditional of all the island groups in Micronesia. Until the early 1970s men walked around town in Yap wearing loincloths while women dressed in grass skirts. Although most have now adopted western clothing, Yapese retain a deep respect for their cultural ways. Women work in the taro patches to produce the staple item of the diet, while men fish. The villages of Yap are tightly organized and ranked according to a caste system, with each village having its own chief and council. In the main islands of Yap, unlike the rest of Micronesia, the patrilineal kin group—the one traced through the father's side—is dominant.

The four thousand people living in the coral atolls near Yap practice a much simpler way of life. They subsist on fish and taro or breadfruit, wear their traditional dress (loincloth and lavalava), and even today carry on the long-distance canoe voyages for which their islands are famous. Like Chuuk, these islands are strongly matrilineal and have a political system that is much weaker than most parts of Micronesia.

Palau (population 20,000). This group of high islands, the largest

Fig. 1. American Jesuit missionary with his people in Chuuk (1978). Courtesy of Micronesian Seminar.

landmass of all Micronesia, shares many of Yap's social and political features. It is divided into villages, or districts, each under the authority of a chief and council. As in Yap, the women traditionally worked in the taro patches while the men gathered the fruits of the sea. Palau, too, is a matrilineal society, but married couples generally resided on the husband's family's estate. In one major respect, however, Yap and Palau differ greatly. Palau has always had the reputation of being the first and fastest island group to modernize. Long before the other islands, it sent off hundreds of young people to school and young adults to find work outside Palau. The intense competition at every level of traditional Palauan society has carried over to the present, helping it modernize as well as it has. Today it is considered the most economically advanced group in Micronesia and forms a separate nation, the Republic of Palau.

The Personal Touch

The Social Map

I sit hunched over a pile of papers on my desk when the telephone rings. I pick it up on the third ring, a bit irritated at the interruption, and an island voice immediately asks "Who is this?" I am annoyed at the insistent demand of the person on the other end of the line and am tempted to slam the phone down. After all, he's the one who called me. He owes me the explanation, not me him. Who are you? I want to shout. And why are you wasting my time like this? But somehow I resist the temptation and identify myself to him. His voice is instantly transformed, from the harsh and demanding tone of a few moments before to something warm and supplicant, even reverential. He knows who I am, I think to myself, and we both relax as the caller begins to offer the customary apologies for infringing on my busy schedule.

Later that week another American who has lived on the island for a few years drops into my office and tells me that he would like to find the money to have Micronesian Seminar do a short educational video. We make videos all the time, several a year, on all kinds of topics—health, economic development, social problems of every description—so I ask him what particular issue this video would address. "Phone courtesy," he answers with a scrunched-up face that betrays his distaste. "I'm sick and tired of picking up the phone only to hear the caller demand to know who I am. These people have to learn how to make calls properly. When someone answers, they should identify themselves and state who they want to talk with. We've had phones on the island for

*years now, and it's high time that people learned some courtesy."
Recalling my own experience earlier in the week and countless
similar calls before that, I smile slightly as I wonder whether it's
worthwhile to try to explain what it took me years to figure out.*

This might be a minor misunderstanding, but it's one repeated
many times over in every part of Micronesia. Common island practice in answering the phone conflicts with what is regarded as proper
phone courtesy by a westerner. When islanders and foreigners interact
with one another, there are bound to be cultural collisions, and this is
simply one of them.

But there's more to the matter than this. Underlying the Micronesian's "rude" response on the phone is a logic that stems from a very
different set of cultural values and attitudes. The incident described
above is no more than the flashpoint at which two cultural fields inter-
sect with one another, the swirling waters revealing the juncture of
two different turbulent cultural currents. The logic of the American's
response to the phone message may be clear, at least to western readers, but the logic behind the Micronesian's demand to know who he's
talking to may need clarification. As we come to understand the logic
behind this, we'll have taken a step toward understanding the cultural framework of the island societies. We'll be in a better position to
appreciate the cultural mind-set out of which Micronesians operate.
And that, at bottom, is the purpose of this book.

Everything is personalized in island society. Everyone has a face
and a history. Even if you're a foreigner, you can't remain on an island
for very long and expect to retain your anonymity; for an islander it's
well nigh impossible. How could this not be the case in such a small
population, numbering between a few thousand on one of the larger
islands and just a couple hundred on one of the small coral atolls? Just
as there are no faces without features, so there are no random events
or what westerners might call acts of nature. What is described here—
which I will call personalization—is one of the most basic themes in
an island culture.

Life on a Micronesian island, then, is the sum total of a series of
interpersonal encounters with people who know one another. There
are no shadowlands in which large numbers of nameless people can
find refuge from these close encounters, no crab holes into which per-

sons can crawl to escape recognition. There is no faceless crowd any-where in Micronesia. Everyone, islander or foreign-born, has a name, a social status, and a link of some sort to everyone else in the com-munity.

A social map is indispensable for Micronesians, who busy them-selves fixing individuals on that map. The people in any setting have to be identified, perhaps not by name but certainly as to whether they are kin or non-kin, whether they are older or younger than oneself, what their social status is. All of this is taken quite seriously in the islands and all of it determines just how one person should respond to another. Only when the individual's identity is plotted on the social map, when I have clarified his relationship with me—as younger or older kin, as social inferior or superior—can he respond to me with confidence. Only then can he adopt the appropriate respect behavior, including marks of verbal respect, toward me. That's why Micronesians often ask "Who are you?" when answering the phone, even before they identify themselves and state the purpose of their call. They want to make sure that they have the social identity of the one responding plotted correctly so that they can answer appropriately.

The social map in just about any part of Micronesia would contain any number of features. There are the traditional residential groups, clusters of houses that form a closely knit extended family group, each headed by an older male in the family. This might be called the inner circle of relationship and it will be dealt with in greater detail in the next chapter. Then there is a broader group of people who live in rather close proximity with one another in what might be loosely called a village. The people in this group, not always closely related by blood or even marriage, might number between a hundred and a thou-sand or more. They are governed by a chief of some sort, but his title and authority vary from one culture to another. In a few island groups, notably Pohnpei and the Marshalls, can be found an additional tier, a cluster of villages governed by a paramount chief. Anyone belonging to any of these concentric circles could, of course, be identified as one of "my people."

But there are other, more complex features to be plotted on the social map. An individual living in a particular village might have members of his extended family group living at the other end of the island, or perhaps on another island altogether. Through his own dispersed extended family members, then, he could easily acquire an affiliation with others residing in this same place. He could find himself tied to them simply because of shared interests, or because of help they provided for his own relatives, or possibly because one of them even became a promised brother or sister to someone in his family. Likewise, his wife's relatives would give him a new set of relationships in those communities to which she had close links.

Overall, any one person might have ties in any number of places, thanks to the dispersal of people he could call relatives by blood or marriage. In short, he could find "his people" just about anywhere. Not only would he be expected to recognize them by tracing the link between them, but he would be required to show each of them the proper deference that his relationship with them called for. The demands imposed on a person by these crosscutting relationships account in good part for the great care that Micronesians take in tracking their pedigree and for the astonishing detail with which they can pinpoint their blood ties with nearly anyone. The average American, who can barely keep track of his second cousins, can only wonder at this feat.

Age is another significant feature on the social map. Ranking by age is taken very seriously in the islands, with deference owed to a brother who is just one year older. In my experience throughout the islands, brothers tend to avoid socializing with one another because of the strict system of respect based on age. When I first appeared at Xavier High School as a young Jesuit scholastic to replace my cousin (our fathers were brothers), who had finished his teaching assignment just before I arrived, my Micronesian students would invariably ask me who was older. When I told them he was, they would follow up with the second question, just as important as the first: Whose father was older? This implied that respect was not simply based on the relative age of the two individuals themselves, but was dependent as well on which of their parents was older. When I answered that my cousin's father was older than mine, the issue was easily resolved: on two counts I was judged inferior to my cousin and so was expected to be deferential to him.

The age-rank question is not always resolved so simply, however. Years ago, when I was director of Xavier High School, one of the brightest students in our senior class began to take a serious academic tumble with just a few months left before graduation. When I called him in one evening, I found that he and his first cousin, a classmate at the school, had a falling out with one another over remarks that his cousin had made about him. Why didn't he talk to his cousin? I asked. He told me that even though he was older than his cousin—something that should have given him the right to redress any personal grievances—he had been told by his mother before he left his island to respect his cousin as his elder. "But he's not your elder," I replied. "You're older than he." He admitted as much before he came in with the clincher: his cousin's mother was older than his own mother. People are ranked, then, not just by their age relative to their siblings, but also by the age of their parents relative to their siblings. In fact, many Micronesians can push this back a generation earlier and tell you what the age rank of each of their grandparents was. Such information is important in the islands because it can determine which branch of the family outranks the others even today. All this is part of the social map.

Newcomers, too, have to be located on the social map somehow if islanders are to have any meaningful contact with them. Micronesians, like others, try to construct a social chain that links them to the person who just presented herself in the office or on the phone. That sixth degree of relationship that supposedly links anyone in the world to just about anyone else is essential in a society that is so highly dependent on personal relationships. I remember walking into a village on a distant island that I had never before visited and encountering a young man whom I had never met. When I told him that I was a Catholic priest working on Pohnpei, he blinked and his face remained unchanged. Only when I mentioned that I had once taught at Xavier did the networking begin, and we soon discovered that I had taught his wife's father during my early years at the school. After that link was made, I found myself on the social map, and he began retelling the horror stories, so often repeated by his in-laws, of my impossible demands during fitness class (thirty push-ups, fifty sit-ups, and one hundred jumping jacks as a starter) and chasing students around the field when they fell behind in their laps. The bond between us was established then and there.

Because being plotted on the social map is a prerequisite for any meaningful exchange with island people, it is not especially helpful when young Americans introduce themselves by their first name and then go silent, as so often happens these days. Whenever I suffer through this abbreviated introduction, I imagine the Micronesian to whom they are introduced thinking, "Oh, that's nice, but who *are* you?" As the American stands there with a smug sense of duty done, the islander is searching for social cues that might allow him to connect with his guests. Who sent them? Where do they work? What ties might they have with his people? Is there anything that he might use as a starting point to establish the connection between him and these people who have appeared in front of him?

Accept me for who I am, the American seems to be insisting, as he offers his first name and whatever visual clues his host can pick up. I can't plot you on my social map, the islander might be thinking, and so I don't know how to connect with you as a person. At bottom, each is looking for the personal touch, but as so often happens in intercultural situations, they're running on entirely different tracks.

There was a time when Americans—or Australians or Europeans—had carefully constructed social maps of their own. When I was growing up in Buffalo during the 1940s, we all knew the names of everyone in our neighborhood and we could have easily recited a list of each one's accomplishments and foibles. We also knew the name of our neighborhood policeman, who was often called on to settle minor family disputes or talk to parents whose child had misbehaved. It wasn't unusual for neighbors to come over to borrow a cup of sugar or a little flour for something they were baking that day. The decline of this type of neighborhood, once common throughout much of the western world, has been well documented by sociologists. On a recent visit to the United States, though, I noticed something that I had never reflected on before—the demise of the front porch. As a child, I would see people sitting out on their porches facing the street engaging in conversation with passersby or the people next door. Now the porches on the old houses were mostly vacant, and houses built after the 1950s, usually without front porches, opened into the backyards. It was there in the backyard, out of sight of the neighbors, where barbecuing was done and socializing took place.

Yet even today in small towns the constellation of personal relationships still rules. Stop in the local luncheonette and listen carefully to the conversation. There, at the mention of a name like Homer, people will know the occupation (*gas station owner*), marital status (*married once but the wife died ten years ago*), what he does for recreation (*poker on Friday nights and deer hunting a few times a year*). If the conversation carried on long enough, they could easily fill in much of his personal history as well (*Do you remember the time old Homer managed to set his beard on fire while trying to light his pipe?*). That's the type of place that most evokes the down-home feel that prevails in Micronesia.

Size of population is a key determinant in how personal the society will be, but it's not the only factor. Rural communities in America, because of their small size, will probably always tend to reflect the personal dimension of life. Autonomy simply doesn't work there: it's hard to imagine anyone in such a community flying under the radar screen. But somehow the personal also seemed to flourish in many parts of Buffalo, a city of over half a million when I was growing up after World War II. We had our own social maps, not for the entire city, but at least for our subsection of the city—our own neighborhood. Social survival in those days seemed to demand that we be on close terms with those who shared the adjacent houses on our street and those on blocks nearby. This was accomplished by splitting the large city into manageable sections, thus allowing personal relations to flourish in this neighborhood area. If this is no longer the case in cities like Buffalo, we can't simply blame the size of the city (indeed, the city today has less than half the population it had then). Other factors may have led to the unconscious decision over time to depersonalize neighborhoods so that they eventually resembled the city at large: a warren of anonymity.

Micronesia, if only because of its limited population and its ready-made "neighborhoods," will continue to prize the personal and value the social map. Besides, the island tradition is too strong to be easily shed. Yet, pressures are operating more strongly today than ever before to contain this personalization as we shall see.

The Faceless Public

Another phone at another desk in another office. When the phone rings, it is the elected governor who picks it up. The governor is a Micronesian, a well-respected young man who has a strong following on his island. He has a U.S. college education with a major in political science, and some years of experience working in the island government at the highest level. He is generally perceived as a rising young star in the political heavens of his new island nation. On top of all this, he has a high-ranking traditional title on his own island.

As he picks up the phone, there is no need for him to consult his social map. The voice at the other end is very familiar. "This is your traditional chief calling," the indignant voice states. The caller then goes on to explain that he has been arrested for use of illegal drugs and that he is phoning the governor from prison. The chief demands that he be released immediately.

The governor pauses only a moment before his reply. "This is not the traditional chief calling. It's Celestino Ambrose, a private citizen. You've been arrested for drug use, and you'll have to serve your time in jail like anyone else." He hangs up with a wry smile before he informs his administrative assistant to make sure that the "chief" is treated like any other prisoner.

The governor's message may have been delivered to prison guards, but they just can't bring themselves to carry it out. The chief is given his own cell, decorated according to his own tastes, and food gifts are brought in so as to spare him the indignity of having to eat the poor prison fare. The prison rules are relaxed to permit him to see visitors any time of the day or night. He is a prisoner, but one treated in a very special way by the guards, who all too readily recognize his privileged status.

This vignette encapsulates the dilemma that Micronesians face today. Do they continue to use their social map and pay the customary respect to those people to whom they are bound, or do they jettison the map and bow to the demands of a democracy in which all are to be treated equally? The governor was clearly prepared to treat the chief as just another citizen, one to be held to account for his crimes just as any other person would, but the jailors couldn't bring themselves to look on the chief as simply another prisoner. Perhaps the governor's education and his previous experience in an American-like government system made it easier for him to adopt his stance. His high traditional title, which gave him cultural status comparable to the chief's, might have encouraged him to treat the chief as he did.

Whatever the case, the dilemma is real and it is enacted dozens of times every day in each of the new island nations of Micronesia. Social maps and the pattern of personal relationships plotted on them are all well and good, modern society is telling Micronesians, but if an island society would like to develop into a successful modern nation it will have to do much better than that. In the end, it will have to get used to dealing with persons as *customers* (in business), as *citizens* (in government), and as *clients* (in public service). It will have to accustom itself to treating its people as a faceless public.

Much of our modern-day western understanding of proper management, after all, derives from the ways bureaucracies operate. Government offices are supposed to be little hives in which functionaries operate according to fixed rules—issuing licenses, collecting taxes, carrying on the other business of government according to mandated guidelines. The regulations governing the conduct of business are clear. So is the authority system and the hierarchical chain of command. The flowcharts taped to the wall of the office tell everything there is to know about the authority system: who can overrule whom in the bureau. Yet, the chain of command in a bureaucracy is not as important as it might seem, for each office constitutes a separate cell with its own distinct procedures and it operates rather autonomously on a day-by-day basis.

The persons who serve in a bureaucracy are specially trained functionaries, apparatchiks without any interest in where we were born, what we do for a living, who our maternal grandparents may be, and what title we might hold. All such information is judged irrelevant, for the bureaucracy is faceless and impersonal. Administrative procedures dictate that all who ask for service, whether high- or low-born, whether penthouse occupant or slum-dweller, are to be treated impartially. All that matters is whether the applicant for service has satisfactorily complied with the regulations that govern the office's conduct of business.

Just as in the theory of a bureaucracy the one requesting service is faceless and formless, so too is the one who delivers the service. The bureaucracy is composed of persons who are selected for their positions solely on the qualifications they possess to perform the work required of them. These functionaries operate like interchangeable parts, not in the sense that any one of them can perform any and all jobs, but in that a person could be replaced by anyone outside the bureaucracy possessing the necessary skills with no impact on the system. Everything would move as efficiently as before.

None of this, of course, is at all compatible with the way in which island life was conducted in the past. Impersonality? Anonymity? Business conducted with a blind eye to social status? Procedural rules first, persons second? Very little resonates with the value system that would have guided traditional conduct. Is it so surprising, then, that few of the business or government offices in Micronesia seem to embody in practice these ideals of bureaucracy? Even on Guam, an island situated on the boundary of Micronesia that has remained under American governance for over a century, a person seeking service routinely will call a *primo,* or cousin, in a government office, no matter what service is required.

What we know as the rules of good management are derived largely from the procedures for bureaucracies, which themselves are of recent North Atlantic vintage. As Max Weber pointed out in his classic work on the subject, bureaucracies are not the historical rule but the exception, even in the mammoth political structures that were erected following the imperial conquests of the Near Eastern, Germanic, and Mongolian empires. The far more common form of administration was through personal legates or court servants, individuals whose authority was temporary and much more open-ended than that of bureaucratic functionaries. In short, bureaucracies and the principles of management that derive from them were not to be found in the great ancient empires of the world nor even in European courts and the political systems that evolved from them. Like other features of our global landscape today—like democratic political institutions and human rights terminology, for instance—the management procedures that we sometimes regard as universal and innate are actually a modern innovation. They are the product of a particular socioeconomic environment, even if they have gained wide acceptance throughout the world today.

The management procedures of bureaucracy have proven their worth, to be sure. They have served the West well, just as they have those societies in other parts of the world that have adopted them. But let's not underestimate the cultural gap between bureaucracy and traditional island practice so as not to make the mistake of assuming that these management procedures can be easily grafted onto any society. Micronesians are going to have to pay a steep cultural price for the efficiency in government and business that strict bureaucratic practice promises to bring their societies.

Again, small population size simply increases the tension between the two systems. In America there is a very small chance of discovering that the police officer who has just pulled you over for speeding is an old friend, or that the judge in your traffic court was a classmate of yours thirty years ago, or that the loan officer in your bank is your in-law or second cousin. In small island societies, on the other hand, the odds are good that you might know your arresting officer or your judge or your loan officer. You can't help running into someone you know in a place as small as a Pacific island, but to do so and not to respond in a culturally appropriate manner, with all that this might imply, is abhorrent. Impersonality is a function of size, not just of attitude, as we have already seen. In other words, it's difficult to look into the faces of people one sees nearly every day and pretend that they are no more than a faceless crowd.

Bureaucracy, along with the modern government and legal systems it undergirds, is built on the assumption that all, no matter who they are or where they are from, no matter how closely they may be related to the one in charge, are equal in the eyes of the law or the government and so should be treated the same. Lady Justice with her scales is represented as a blindfolded woman, indifferent to the face or background of those she serves. In an office, all who seek assistance enter through the front door and queue up in front of the desk, with applications judged on their own merit.

But in a highly personalized society, can any assumption be more misleading? Lady Justice peeks through her blindfold at times, and the office manager lets customers slip in the back door and puts the application forms of some favored persons at the top of the stack on his desk. Personalization trumps in the islands, even in business, politics, and government service—areas that should in theory be managed according to the code of the impersonal bureaucracy.

An even-handed, blindfolded approach to just about anything—business investment licenses, bank loans, or court procedures—will be

Fig. 2. Islanders on Guam waiting in line to register (1955). Courtesy of Peabody Museum, Harvard.

a special challenge to Micronesian societies, as it would be in many developing countries throughout the world. But the smallness of Pacific island societies only exacerbates the problem—not only because it is harder to resist the temptation to help a relative or friend (since they are everywhere), but also because departures from the bureaucratic norm are more easily detected in such places and so "corruption" is much more easily exposed.

Reforms are urged by international financial institutions to bring these societies in line with "best practice" and expectations of the modern world. But somehow the reforms are sidelined, or perhaps sluggishly and halfheartedly implemented, or, more rarely, even rejected outright in a gesture of defiance. As this happens time and again, the confidence of the western world in the Micronesian island states begins to wane. The insistent demands become stronger for the islands to surrender their social maps and do what the rest of the developed world has done: embrace bureaucracy and the concept of the faceless crowd. Let the features of that traditional world, populated by chiefs, in-laws, lineage mates, older and younger siblings, and senior family members, blur to such a point that they are no longer recognizable.

So, from telephone courtesy to the procedures associated with good government, island societies find themselves in a strange position. They are handicapped by the personalization that is so much a part of island society. Ironically, the very quality that makes Micronesians so charming in the eyes of the western world also hinders them from achieving the development and governance goals that are being held up for them. This personalization may go a long way in melting the hearts of tourists, but it is perceived as a stumbling block for good government and earns the new island societies a poor rating on the international index. Such are the dilemmas of development that Micronesian countries face in their transition from small personalized societies to western-style nations.

«·«·« 2 »·»·»

Forging an Identity

The Social Identity

*A high school senior from an outer island school comes in to talk
with an American teacher about her plans after graduation. The
teacher wants the girl, who is a bright student, to go to college
in the United States, but the girl tells her teacher that her mother
wants her to stay at home so that she can be with her younger
sister and help take care of two cousins who are coming to the
island to begin high school next year. The mother has other objec-
tions to her daughter going off to college—she thinks that the
daughter ought to have other family members around to watch
over her.*

*The American teacher reacts strongly to this. "Why won't
your mother let you lead your own life?" she asks, obviously frustrated that the girl is going to endanger her own academic career
so that she can provide for her family. The teacher promises to
help the girl find a college and the scholarship money the girl
needs. She points out to the girl that if she postpones her schooling, she might lose interest in her education, get married, and
never have another opportunity to get her college degree. That
would seriously limit her choices in the future. The girl listens
to her teacher, drops her eyes, and sighs. For a moment she says
nothing, and then she mutters, "But my family needs my help."*

*The American teacher has exhausted her options so she says
good-bye to the girl and leaves the school office. Outside, she sees
a group of girls, wearing lavalavas and decorative palm fronds
around their necks and on their wrists, as they prepare to practice*

*one of the dances for graduation next month. The teacher pauses
for a moment as she watches the girls fall into line and begin the
rhythmic hand and hip motions of the dance, each girl's move-
ments coordinated to all the others. That's such a good image of
what life is like out here, she thinks. Each individual, no matter
who she is or what she can do, blends in with the group so effort-
lessly that sometimes she seems to have no soul of her own.*

This American teacher was not the first visitor to the islands to
have entertained such thoughts. Albert Sturges, an early American
missionary to Pohnpei, wrote a line a century and a half ago that
might have echoed the sentiments of many other foreign visitors to
the islands before and since. "Humanity here is one viscous mass,"
Sturges wrote, "and there is no such thing here as individual action
or individual responsibility." Sturges undoubtedly would have written
the same line if he had been in Yap or Palau or anywhere else in the
region.

Everyone knows of numerous instances when islanders have fallen
into line and marched off as a group to do something that a number of them as individuals might not have chosen to do. Young men
gather for drinking bouts on weekends. Girls, like the one in the story
above, stay at home to take care of the family, no matter how strong
the personal desire to go on to college. Family members work all day
to prepare the food that they will take to a long customary meeting
that evening even if they would prefer to join friends somewhere else.
To Americans and other outsiders this kind of behavior betrays what
they might call the herd mentality: Micronesians thundering off in a
single direction regardless of the consequences. To their mind, this
group-oriented behavior is just further evidence that Micronesians are
always ready to put aside their own preferences in order to fit in with
the group. For all their friendliness and good-natured charm, islanders seem to be an embodiment of the old caricature: people who "go
along in order to get along." If cultures were plotted on a scale from
individualistic to group-minded, island societies would always run off
the latter end of the scale.

Indeed, it is difficult to exaggerate the importance of an islander's
social identity. The Micronesian is first and foremost a member of a
social group. "I am because we are" is the often-quoted Bantu proverb

to express the importance of the family in Africa. Micronesians would proclaim a loud amen to that. Indeed, all that any islander had ever become would have stemmed from this social identity, and so group maintenance was always to be preferred to individual achievement. From the arrival of the first settlers to the islands, the cultural system was always tilted in this direction. A person's livelihood in old island society depended entirely on land that belonged to the family group. To the extent that he retained membership in this family group, he could access the resources he needed to live off in the future. Even personal prestige, much of which was inherited through bloodlines, was largely dependent on his membership in a family. Tight family cohesion, of course, was essential if its members were to succeed in a traditional society, just as harmony was a critical element for survival at the village and island level. Fitting in, then, even at the expense of personal satisfaction, was demanded of islanders if their social groups and their society as a whole were to function properly.

At the heart of the identity of an islander is the "family"—a term with a broad range of meanings throughout the various cultures of the islands. It is a word that could be understood in a number of ways even within a single culture. The "family" that strikes the deepest roots, the meaning that explains the grounding of an islander's identity, is not the western-style nuclear family consisting of mother, father, and children. Neither is it what foreigners frequently refer to as the "clan." The clan is composed of hundreds and hundreds of people, usually spread over several islands; its members don't interact regularly and many of them don't know one another at all. When we move to the middle ground between the two, a descent group anthropologists call the lineage, we are getting closer to that fuzzy concept that many refer to as the "extended family." In just about all Micronesian societies, the lineage is the fundamental family unit. Nearly everywhere, it descends from an older woman and includes all her children and the children of her daughters. Hence, the lineage is heavily weighted toward the women of the group and so is called a matrilineage.

The lineage is a very small branch of a clan; it might be three or even four generations deep and include anywhere between ten and thirty persons. An islander might identify himself as a member of a lineage, using this as his identity tag. But even a lineage is not adequate for defining a person's group membership because the cluster of close relatives around a person include a number of people who formally belong to another lineage. One's spouse and sometimes children would be among those outside one's lineage. After all, a person's mother and father must necessarily be from different lineages since marriage within the lineage is forbidden. So, the nebulous "extended family" group with whom a person most closely associates is a mixed group—some belonging to that person's own lineage and some with other ties even though they are not members of one's lineage.

The extended family worked the land together and ate together. They entertained together and would have at one time probably shared a canoe house. They shared responsibility for raising children, especially during their younger years. They apportioned work responsibilities on the land. They looked after the resources—land and houses and tools—that were needed for daily life. They did all these things under the banner of the basic lineage around which they were gathered.

Lineages extended outward, becoming branches in a clan, a multigenerational tree rooted in some woman who was long dead. The clan is broad and disparate, its members scattered over a wide geographical expanse, and so it functions more as another identity marker than anything else. Yet, membership in a clan serves as a person's passport in a journey to another island, or even to a remote part of his own island. In the past, people traveling to a distant place had merely to identify themselves by their clan and they might expect to receive hospitality from members of the same clan. Lodging and food were usually provided to the visitors as long as they were on island. Even today, Micronesians often avail themselves of this kind of assistance. But they also use their clan to provide other help. One Chuukese woman, for instance, tells of her experience as a young woman when she was frightened by a drunken teenager who was bothering her. Instead of turning to her husband for help, she spoke to a clansman from another island, a strong young man with a reputation as something of a street fighter. The young man confronted the drunk and told him that he would be protecting the woman from his clan, thus ending the trouble quickly. Islanders may not have much to do with their clansmen on a regular basis, but members of their clan remain a resource to turn to when need arises.

Personal names are significant in Micronesia, but the way in which they have changed over the years may offer a window on how identities are also changing. The last name emerged over the past century, especially during the postwar years. At first the person was identified by her own island name or Christian name (e.g., Birigita), but in official church or school records she might be further identified by her village (e.g., Birigita from Sapore). In time, it became fashionable for individuals to take their father's name as their family name (Birigita Nicolas, for instance), as has been done for centuries in Europe. The father's name could be that of the natural father or the adoptive father—and well over half of all Micronesians were adopted a generation or two ago. Consequently, the last name could switch back and forth, to the consternation of newcomers like me. In a very few places, notably Yap, the person might use the Christian name as a first name and the island name as something of a last name. The practice of passing down genuine last names over several generations, as in the western world, began with mixed bloods with names like Heine, Hartmann, Hofschneider, Hadley, or Hashiguchi. It is becoming more widespread with each generation, as last names become de rigueur.

The last name, handed down on the father's side according to western custom, may be a symbol of the growing strength of the patrilineal in island society. The identity of the "family" was once embodied in the lineage, with descent passing down the mother's side, as we have seen. But the increasing use of the father's last name offers another, different way of identifying the "family" of an individual. (Most of us westerners, of course, continue to take our father's last name as our own.) Today it can be considered more a counterweight to the old matrilineal system than a direct challenge to it.

And yet, a counterweight to the matrilineal descent group is nothing new. Nearly everywhere in Micronesia a child was always linked to a web of relationships on his father's side as well as his mother's. As he grew up, he stood to benefit from both, especially through access to land and other resources, just as he incurred obligations to both. His identity, though drawn from both sides, was more closely dependent on his mother's lineage than his father's. Perhaps more important than anything else, his mother's lineage always remained a final fallback for him if everything went wrong. If he was judged unacceptable by his father's lineage, if he failed in school and in business, or if his wife and children left him, he could count on always being accepted by his own lineage—his mother's family. His matrilineage—the core of his extended family—was his origin, his most basic source of identity, and the final refuge for him when he was rejected everywhere else. More than anywhere else, this is where home was for an islander. This was, in the most fundamental sense, one's family.

The Price of Alienation

Tomaso was just nineteen years old when he took his own life. He had been a good, hard-working boy, always ready to help in gathering food or doing household chores, his family acknowledged. His death was a great shock to everyone in his family.

Tomaso had run out of the house in tears the night of his death, his mother recalled. Shortly before that, an argument had broken out between Tomaso and his father after his father had refused Tomaso's request for the money he needed to attend a church-sponsored youth picnic. Tomaso's mother would go no further in speaking about the events of that evening, however. It was a visitor staying with the family who described the conversation between Tomaso and his father just before Tomaso left the house in tears. Tomaso, he said, sulked for a few moments after his father turned down his request before he began a long recital of other times that his father had refused to help him. At the end of it all, the boy shook his head violently and muttered, "What am I doing here if you don't have any love for me?" Then he ran off sobbing. They found his body early the next morning hanging from one of the lower branches of a breadfruit tree three hundred yards behind the family house.

Tomaso's tragedy is a story that has been repeated hundreds of times over, throughout the past four decades. Since 1970 there have been more than 1,500 recorded suicides in Micronesia, most of them similar in many respects to that of Tomaso. Some of the suicide victims have taken their lives when they were refused small requests like his—a white shirt for graduation, a few dollars for an outing with friends, or permission to use the family car. In some cases, young men ended their lives when their families refused to accompany them to ask for the hand of the girl they wanted to marry. But not all suicides were

Fig. 3. Family on an atoll near Pohnpei (1952). Courtesy of United Nations.

precipitated by such refusals. Often enough, the victim might have been smarting from a scolding he had received from an elder in the family—frequently one of his parents, but occasionally from an older brother, an uncle, or even a grandparent. In many of these cases, as in Tomaso's, the incident that took place immediately before the suicide was just the latest in a series of conflicts that might have made the victim wonder whether his family loved him. After all, in Micronesian societies love implied a willingness to nurture an individual, primarily through food in traditional times, but increasingly today through generosity with money and other resources.

But not all suicides were prompted by the refusal of a request or a scolding by the family. There have been dozens of persons who ended their lives because of their shame at something they themselves had done to hurt their families. One ten-year-old boy who disobeyed his father's orders to be home early in the evening hanged himself for fear of what his father would say when he returned. A young man in another place took his own life after he had ruined the family car that he had taken out one evening without permission. Another young man, who had been carrying on a sexual affair with his first cousin, hanged himself when her pregnancy began to show. In each of these cases, and the dozens of similar ones, the victim was well aware that he had done something to offend his family, and that this would bring with it not just retribution but, even more important, alienation from his family.

Nowhere is the importance of the family so strongly underscored as in the phenomenon of suicide. Whether the victim felt that he had wronged his family or had been wronged by them, the underlying cause for suicide in the vast majority of cases is a perceived rupture between the individual and his family. Thus, we might infer that in the eyes of Micronesians it is broken bonds with one's family more than anything else that makes life *not* worth living. Loss of a job, failure in school, personal disgrace, or even the death of a loved one will seldom lead to suicide in the islands. It's not easy to persuade western-trained psychologists of this, so convinced are they that clinical depression, often brought on by personal failure, is at the core of the suicide problem everywhere. They cling to the notion that financial hardship or loss of opportunity, the dead ends in life that can bring on depression among their own people, must be responsible for the same in the islands. They assume that what is true of suicide in the West must also be true in Micronesia.

What they miss, however, is the central place that family membership plays in the identity of an individual. Social identity is the bedrock of one's existence; it is the basis for what westerners might call self-esteem. It is central in a way that one's individual achievements or abilities can never be. Notwithstanding American psychology books on the subject, a sense of personal worth for an islander is grounded in knowing that one has a secure place in the family.

Suicide has a long history in the islands. There are stories of individuals who, feeling unwanted by their families, hopped into a canoe and put out to sea to drift off until they perished. Although the method might differ, the psychological strategy is akin to what occurs today when a young man ties a rope around his neck and drifts off into anoxia and death. There are touching tales, romanticized over the years, of young lovers leaping off a cliff together when their love seemed doomed. The classic is the legend of the two lovers on Guam, in which the couple bound their hair together before making the leap into the sea. These stories make good tourist tales, Pacific island versions of Romeo and Juliet. But they disguise in favor of the romantic element what was in all likelihood the real motive for the suicide—the fear of alienation from their families. In the past, young couples who were forbidden permission to marry one another had other ways of resolving their problem. They could, for instance, acquiesce in their parents' wishes and marry other partners, meanwhile working to sabotage their marriages and so send signals to their parents that they were meant for one another. The usual strategy seems to have been to conduct an affair with one another even as they were married to other partners until they had shamed their spouses into divorcing them.

Even so, suicide today is gradually changing to reflect newer social patterns. There has always been a great preponderance of males among suicide victims: well over 90 percent of all victims are male, and over two-thirds of these are young men between the ages of fifteen and thirty. In Palau and the Marshall Islands especially, but increasingly in other places as well, more males are taking their own lives because of a problem with a girlfriend or wife. Suicide, which at one time was employed as a desperate measure to cope with the loss of family, is now sometimes motivated by the loss of a loved one outside the blood family. Perhaps this signals a redefinition of family to include spouses and others outside the bloodline in the eyes of today's Micronesians.

Whether today or in the past, suicide has always offered us an understanding of what makes life unlivable in the islands: loss of a respected place in the family. Conversely, it is today, as it always has been, a clear indication of how central the family is to an islander's identity and meaning in life. "I am because we are," as the Bantu saying goes. To take this saying a step further, we might conclude that the "I" without a strong link to the "we" is pointless.

Over the past four decades, the Federated States of Micronesia, Palau, and the Marshall Islands have lost an average of forty persons a year to suicide, most of them young males. Suicide has been the main cause of death for people in this cohort of the population. As we have seen, the suicide problem is strongly linked to the importance islanders accord to their social identity and the enormous role that family plays in their lives. We might, then, pose these questions: Will the suicide problem in the islands be resolved only as the social identity is altered, the role of the family is diminished, and the shift to a more individual frame of reference takes place? But, if the "we" gives place to the "I," what further problems will this create for people who are long accustomed to subordinating their own personal interests to the good of the social group?

Land: Symbol and Reward of Identity

"Mama," the girl asked, "Why is Uncle Julio going to court again today to argue about that piece of land? We're not even using it for anything except for the coconut trees someone planted there a long time ago. Why not just let those other people have it if they need it?"

Her mother paused for a moment to collect her thoughts and check her emotions, but even as she spoke her eyes revealed her strong feelings. She told her daughter how the family had first acquired the land a long time ago, long before she was even born. She described how her father, now dead, used to visit the land once or twice a week to make copra there. Her younger brother, she recalled, would sometimes accompany her father to help him cut the copra and dry it in the shed they set up on their property. When they returned, she told her daughter, the two of them would talk on and on about what they had done that day and what they planned to do on their next visit. That was the land that had provided the copra they sold for cash to pay for the little things the family needed, she told her daughter.

She also told her daughter that the land had a name, a name the daughter had never heard before. That little piece of land had a history, her mother told her daughter, and the history was a part of the family. Then her eyes moistened as she reminded her daughter that on that little piece of land her own mother was buried.

In the past land stood for everything that made it possible for people to survive in an island culture. Land was the resource without which no one could live. It meant the plot of earth on which people could plant their crops and harvest from their trees, but it also included rights to offshore flats and submerged reefs that could be used for fishing. "Land," in its broad sense, included all that was once necessary for food cultivation, housing, canoe making, medicine, and production of tools. That's why Chuukese have long called land "our strength, our life, our hope for the future."

Access to land was generally passed on to people through their family. The way in which this was done is too complex to describe here (anthropologists have written volumes on land tenure in different parts of Micronesia), but we can say that the rights to use land were handed down to persons through the extended family, either the father's lineage or the mother's. There were cases in which a piece of land was given to an individual outright for his valor in warfare or for an outstanding contribution to the chief, but this was always very much the exception rather than the rule. In general, then, the traditional system was set up in such a way as to provide a person with what he needed to sustain himself throughout life—but on condition that he remained a member of the family group that possessed rights to the land. Access to land was one of the major rewards of membership in the family.

If land was a reward for family affiliation, it was also a symbol of family solidarity. In some parts of Micronesia—Yap, for instance—individuals and families took their names from the land. In island groups where this was not done, the link between the individual and the family by way of the land could be symbolized in other ways. In Chuuk and the Central Carolines, the umbilical cord of the newborn baby was buried on his lineage land, suggesting that the child sprang from the land. At death the person would customarily be buried on the lineage land, regardless of where the person's spouse was interred. The meaning was clear: just as the individual springs from the family land, he returns to the same land at death. Men and women may come and go, but the land endures—the same land that serves as the marker par excellence for the identity of the family group or lineage.

Land is a symbol of collective identity. Land is a marker of the extended family. Land is the element that binds generations of family to one another. Land is the source and the final resting place for the individual. Land is the identification tag for the individual. All this goes a long way in explaining why such a mystique of land is to be found throughout the Pacific. In former times land was not just a possession, but a part of one's social being. Land was as inalienable as, say, an arm or a leg. It could at times be taken away by force or as a punishment, but land was never regarded as a mere commodity.

If this was the traditional mystical meaning of land, there are signs that this meaning is changing today. The first of these signs is that land disputes now clog courts everywhere in Micronesia. Disputes over ownership of parcels of land are nothing new in the islands, but today's disputes challenge the very principles that have always governed land inheritance. One of the most common occurs when the head of a lineage, who is supposed to represent the interests of this land-holding group, passes a piece of land over to one of his own sons. As lineage head, the man should be speaking on behalf of the entire lineage and so getting approval of each adult member of his extended family before he disposes of any land. The land should be used to benefit the members of his lineage, including his sisters' children, rather than his own. His own children, after all, do not belong to his lineage, but to his wife's. Instead, as the nuclear family becomes ever more dominant and his interest in his own sons outweighs his concern for his sisters' children, the man often dismisses the claim of his extended family or lineage over the land in order to aid his own children. In doing this, he not only betrays his lineage and all that it would have represented to him in the past, but he is also generating conflict between his own children and their first cousins over rights to the land that he has passed on to the former. Hostility between relatives is bound to mount as the dispute lingers on in the court system over the years.

Another sign of change with respect to land is the frequency with which it is being sold today. Heads of families in Pohnpei and Chuuk were selling parcels of land thirty or forty years ago for the cash they need to purchase a pickup truck as the road extended to their village. Others were offering land in exchange for the debts they had accumulated at stores on the islands, so that store owners had become major landowners in many island groups. Land, which was never regarded by traditional islanders as a simple commodity, was certainly becoming one under the impact of the cash economy. Land might have been the one resource needed for survival on the islands at one time, but money was rapidly replacing it as the single most useful resource.

The growing importance of the cash economy, along with the nuclear family that it has helped spawn, has eroded some of the symbolic importance of land among islanders today. Land has been commodified to an extent that older Micronesians could have never imagined, and the nuclear family has weakened some of the traditional links between land and the identity of the extended family. The meaning of land is clearly changing, but this is happening more slowly than might be expected. Meanwhile, land retains a value to Micronesians that goes beyond the utilitarian. The number and intensity of conflicts over land everywhere in the islands today attest to the importance of land and the strong emotional response it can arouse.

Land is still a marker of social identity, even if the social unit is changing from the extended family to a smaller unit. Even allowing for the growing sale of parcels of land in exchange for cash in recent years, most islanders still feel a repugnance to selling land. For all the change that has occurred, it might not be too much of an exaggeration to think of a land sale as similar to parlaying a body part into money. Old practices and the habits of thought that support them die slowly, as we know.

For Micronesians to think of land as little more than a negotiable commodity would require a profound change, a much deeper one than has been made up to now. Yet, here again, the formulas for development offered by the West urge islanders to make this change. Economic growth needed to sustain the island nations in the future may demand the sale or long-term lease of land for development purposes, islanders are told. But, despite the inroads that modernization has already made in the islands, people have difficulty subscribing to formulas like this because of the symbolic meaning that land retains for them. Micronesians will not easily be persuaded to offer land as just one more item in the marketplace as long as land is still associated with social identity.

«•«•« 3 »•»•»

Limits of the Individual

Privacy and Personal Choice

The new Peace Corps Volunteer had been on his site, an island of a few hundred people, for just under a month. The romance of island life and a strange culture had worn off quickly. He found his goodwill tested by the ways in which his host family was taking advantage of him. His personal belongings had been opened during his first week on the island, and he had found one or two things missing. How could they presume to rummage through his personal belongings like that, he wondered. Then there was the annoyance of the kids in his host family, especially the two young boys, nine and twelve, who were with him all the time. The boys were lots of fun and their magical smiles lit up the house. But he needed time to be by himself for a while, to think his own thoughts and escape the tight confinement of the family circle.

One afternoon he slipped away from his host family and walked to the far end of the island, not too far off on an island as small as this but hidden from view by some large coral boulders. There he sat on the sand, shielded by the rocks, as he opened his journal and began to ponder what to write. He couldn't have been sitting there for much longer than ten minutes when he glanced up and noticed them. The two boys, wearing a concerned look rather than their usual smile, stood silent for a moment or two before one of them said: "Mama sent us down here to watch you. She's afraid that you might hurt yourself."

It wasn't until months later, when he had a chance to swap stories with other volunteers that the young American under-

37

*stood what the boys meant. As he listened to other similar tales,
it occurred to him that their host families had not yet absorbed
the Americans' need for getting away from other people and
escaping into their own thoughts. For a person to wander off by
himself to find solitude was so unusual that people regarded it as
a warning signal for depression, psychological imbalance, or even
self-destruction.*

Privacy clearly does not have the same value in Micronesian eyes
that it has for westerners. This is the first lesson learned by Americans
who make their home in the islands for any length of time. I can still
see the pairs of eyes peering through the windows as I did my daily
exercises in the plywood house that served as my temporary home in
the village. They belonged to the children who lined up outside the
house every afternoon to enjoy the spectacle. Just as there was no privacy in the village, there were no secrets either, I soon learned. People
were quick to ask me how I was feeling the morning after I made a
rushed trip to the woods to vomit up my dinner in what I naively pre-
sumed was secrecy.

In a traditional island setting, privacy was virtually impossible.
Extended family members piled into dwellings, mats were unrolled
on the floor, and persons slept anywhere they could find floor space.
Food was available in cook pots or perhaps wrapped in banana leaves
to be eaten whenever a person felt hungry. Even clothes, like so much
else in daily life, were often shared by other family members when
need arose. Everyone knew when the young girls in the family began
menstruating (on many islands they were once secluded in menstrual
houses during this part of their cycle), and most of the village was
aware of which boys were sleeping with what girls. But how could
they not have been? Village life was too confined to permit anything
resembling privacy, and family life even more so.

It might appear, then, that Micronesian disdain for privacy is simply making a virtue of necessity. But there is more to the matter than
this. Even today, when housing styles have changed and homes are
equipped with private bedrooms, the island preference for group living seems to trump the desire for privacy. Young people, and even the
not so young, often feel more comfortable huddling four or five to a
room rather than sleeping in different rooms. People may travel alone

at times, if necessity dictates, but their strong preference is to remain in the company of others, especially when visiting new places.

Years ago on Pohnpei, the government started a summer program for at-risk youth; the program, which was intended to challenge these young people, provided a series of exercises designed to test the mettle of the participants. Each year at the conclusion of the program, the young participants were asked which part of the program they found most challenging. Invariably the island participants would say that the hardest test was the two-day solo in the woods—more trying than having to rappel down a sheer eight-hundred-foot cliff, or being thrown into deep water with hands and legs tied to float for an hour or two. In this exercise they were given a little food and sent off to live entirely alone for two days and two evenings. For these young islanders prolonged solitude proved more disturbing than dangerous tests of their physical stamina.

In all my years in the islands I never recall hearing a Micronesian say that he had to be alone to clear his head. If trouble arises, if emotional difficulties beset someone, that person is more likely to find refuge with the family than in solitude. After all, it is the family that has nurtured the person, and it is with the family that the individual finds the emotional support needed to carry on.

As I used to tell my students at Xavier, great fans of western movies that they were, a Micronesian western is simply inconceivable unless the islands were to undergo a radical value change. The hero in the old westerns might come into town, survive a series of trials on behalf of the townspeople or perhaps just to settle old scores, but I could never imagine a Micronesian saddling his horse (metaphorically speaking), giving a tug on the reins, and then galloping off alone to resume a solitary life somewhere over the next mountain ridge.

If privacy is limited in a world in which the social identity is paramount, the range of personal choices will be just as limited. And so it is for Micronesians, for whom individual satisfaction must be sacrificed in favor of the good of the social group. The bright high school senior may have to postpone her college to help her family, as we have seen in the last chapter. If at some later date she does go off to college, the one she will attend may depend not just on where she is accepted and how costly the tuition is, but on the family agenda. She could be called on to assist a married sister in the United States who has several

children, or to remain within a short plane ride from her own island if
her mother's health is failing. She could be summoned back from college at any time if there is a crisis in the family or if one of her relatives
should die. In the past her future husband would have probably been
chosen by elders in the family, but even today her choice in the matter
might be sharply curtailed inasmuch as her family is expected to have
some say in the matter and certainly to bestow final approval. The
children she bears might not necessarily be raised by her, especially if
she has a close relative who is childless. Her parents themselves might
choose to adopt one of her children if all their own children are fully
grown. Needless to say, her career will be dependent on the usual factors that are taken into account in deciding whether a woman will take
a job or not. But it doesn't end there. If she's living on her own island,
other voices, reflecting the needs of a number of family members, will
have to be heard. She might end up taking a job in order to help provide for a sick relative who needs to be referred to the Philippines for
medical treatment. Or she might have to turn down an attractive job
offer to help with the household chores of a sister or a cousin.

The woman's options are limited because of the social ties that
bind her. Male or female, an islander recognizes this as part of the
price of cultivating the social identity with all that it brings. Indeed,
Micronesians may be better off than most westerners in that they at
least recognize the limitations on their freedom of choice and have
made their peace with the need to yield to the family some of their
rights. Westerners, on the other hand, often have unrealistic notions of
the range of their personal choice. In actual fact, accidents of time and
place narrow our options on even such life-altering decisions as where
we live, how we spend our lives, and whom we marry. Happenstance
and dumb luck may account for much of what we attribute to choice.
Micronesians, by contrast, are under no illusion that their own decisions will determine the direction of their lives.

Individual Rights

*When I ran into Teruo standing on the dock ready to hop into his
boat and head for home, we had not seen one another for several
years. "How are you?" I asked him. "How is everything back
home?" This was nothing more than a conventional greeting, so*

I was surprised when he shook his head and launched into a long recital of everything that was going wrong on his island.

Since the elections two months ago, he said, his village had been terribly divided. The contest between the two candidates for mayor had been so bitterly contested that bad feelings persisted between the candidates and their supporters ever since. One of the churches had lost half its congregation, he told me, because its pastor was known to be a staunch supporter of one of the candidates. Fights still broke out at times between young men on different sides. The village was in turmoil, he said, and no one knew when the bad feelings would subside and peace would be restored.

But he went on to tell me that worst of all was the tension within extended families themselves. "Brothers are at war with one another," as he put it. They refused to eat together, work together, or even speak with one another. Meanwhile, the rest of the family was drawn into the conflict, as sisters-in-law shouted at one another and the children in the family made threatening gestures at children whose parents were supporters of the other faction. "If the families can't stay united, what hope do we have?" he lamented.

"It was altogether different in the old days," he told me. I asked him if he meant before political elections were introduced to the islands in early days of the trusteeship.

"No," he said. "Even ten or twenty years ago we had no real problem at election time." He explained that in those days the head of the family gathered everyone before an election and instructed the members of the family how they were to cast their votes. Sometimes the family voted en bloc for one candidate; at other times votes were parceled out to different candidates according to the obligation that the family had to each. But today the head of the family can no longer apportion the votes this way.

When I asked him why not, he just shook his head and stood silent for a moment. Then he blurted out a single word: "Rights." I wasn't sure I understood, so he explained: "Nowadays, our people want to claim their own right to vote. 'One person, one vote,' they say. That's what they're learning in school, and that's what the modern government wants."

Soon after the United States assumed administration of Micronesia as a U.N. trust territory at the end of World War II, the vote was introduced to islanders. Through formal elections the U.S. administration of the islands intended to offer people control over their political leaders for the first time. American officials would have been surprised to know just how much influence islanders already had over chiefs, who, though never elected by the people, depended greatly on their people's support. After all, voting individuals in and out of office is not the only way of keeping the political reins in the people's hands. Long ago an unpopular chief in Pohnpei, who had repeatedly ignored the wishes of his people, found himself abandoned by his people as he went to war against another chiefdom and was slain by his enemies. In Palau unpopular chiefs might be killed outright, sometimes by their own kinsmen. There is good reason why, in the Marshallese language, people are called the "strength" (*kajur*) of the chief. Without them the chief would have been powerless, as he knew very well.

Yet, democracy (rule by the people) in its western form had to have elections. Thus, it was understood that each person was to have a vote in the choice of elected officials in the new island government. The right of the individual to vote, in the eyes of any American, was sacred. What was not always understood, at least by the early U.S. administrators, is that the head of the family often took it upon himself to instruct the family members on how they were to cast that vote. The result might not have been what was intended by island administrators, or by the political theorists of two centuries ago who wrote the vote into the constitutions of the West, but it worked well enough. Today, on the other hand, as family members increasingly vote as individuals, they may be fulfilling the purpose of the ballot, but they can also create serious rifts within the family that cannot be easily healed. Harmful fallout from elections has troubled other villages and islands, as it did Teruo's in the vignette above. The vote is taken very seriously everywhere in Micronesia today, thus accounting for the strong emotions displayed at election time. Ironically, the blessings bestowed by one form of the democratic process (the vote) have been quite mixed. The most modern isn't always the best, as we have seen before and shall see again. Sometimes there are traditional means that accomplish the same general purpose—in this case, people's exercise of control over leaders—but without some of the negative side effects that modern individual-centered practices might bring about.

Another right, generally thought to be as sacred as the right to vote is the right to exercise control over one's own body. What, after all, could be more intimately associated with the individual than the right to control one's own sexuality? Yet, even this was accorded, at least in part, to the family in traditional Micronesian societies. Marriage partners were often assigned to the young, so that even what we today consider the most intimate parts of the corporeal realm were overseen by others. Indeed, sexual access to women in the family was often granted by the head of the family to guests, while wives of absent family members were customarily entrusted to the care, and the sexual intimacies, of older brothers. Moreover, in some island cultures wives of older brothers were often expected to provide sexual initiation for their adolescent brothers-in-law. What could it possibly have meant to declare that a person ought to enjoy control over one's body in those days?

Much of this, of course, has changed today. Arranged marriages are rare, and the sexual intimacies that were once imposed on the women in the family are now largely self-chosen. The Micronesian woman today has far more control over her own sexual activity than ever before. But the expansion of freedom for women has had a downside that has not always been acknowledged. Present-day problems like rape and serious spouse abuse would have been more effectively checked when the woman was under the direct control of her family. Rape, for instance, was rare in the past because anyone violating a woman would have to answer to her family, and retribution could be quick and severe. Just a few years ago the rape of a Yapese girl resulted in the hospitalization of her two teenage assailants.

Moreover, even married women remained under the protective eye of their families. Physical mistreatment by a husband that today would be called spouse abuse was punished by the woman's blood relatives, usually much more effectively than by law enforcement officials and the court system today. One young woman I knew, who was living with her longtime boyfriend, started appearing in public with bruises on her face. She was hesitant to talk about what was happening to her, as most Micronesian women would, no matter how many times I pressed her on the matter. Within a few weeks the problem was solved,

Fig. 4. Young Chuukese woman (1975). Courtesy of Roland Rauchholz.

I heard, when her brother, armed with a baseball bat, appeared in her house and confronted her boyfriend. Villagers joked afterward about the speed with which the boyfriend, still only half-dressed, dashed out of the house and dove into the lagoon to escape retribution at the hands of his girlfriend's brother.

What might appear to a westerner today to be non-negotiable rights in our own place and era clearly were not such in the islands in the past. The claims of the individual in a traditional Micronesian society were certainly restricted. Yet, the protection that the society offered achieved some of the same ends as the rights that are so strongly endorsed today, as we have seen in the examples of control over political authority and control over one's body. In some cases it did this much more effectively, since the family and society had built-in enforcement mechanisms that are often absent today.

Most Pacific cultures employed the same devices for ensuring the respect of the human person and providing what each one needed for a decent life. Mechanisms were established to safeguard the legitimate claims of those without power, usually by placing them under the protection of others, sometimes through adoption or by fashioning a client relationship with those who could provide for them. Micronesians have strong traditions of compassion and respect. I have often seen islanders melt when observing a person in real need, whether that person might need a place to stay for a month, a loan of hundreds of dollars, or a job to feed his family.

One of the toughest men I knew in Chuuk told me that once when visiting Tijuana, Mexico, he saw some youth scavenging in garbage cans for something to eat. He left the cantina in which he was eating, opened his wallet and handed the kids a twenty-dollar bill. His response was typical of the people with whom I have been working all these years. If directly challenged, he might have responded in the old warrior mode; but when faced with those who made no claims upon him except by virtue of their need, he responded with characteristic Pacific largesse. This is the Pacific way.

The language of human rights, on the other hand, is a recent western invention. For most of human history, in the West as in the Pacific, society has been regarded as static and hierarchical. The prevailing social ethic in such societies was grounded on the individual's duties to society, rather than on what one might expect to receive from others. Any formal rights that individuals possessed were linked to their status rather than to their personhood as such. The king had certain rights because of his title, as did the lord of the manor, and even the father of a family. But the simple farmer or serf was protected only by contracts with his social superiors. By and large, the powerless had to depend solely on the sense of fairness and compassion of others.

With the development of modern Europe emerged individualism. This was partly an outgrowth of the self-consciousness of the Enlightenment, but even more a reaction to the development of the modern nation-state, which posed a greater threat to the individual than the ancient society ever did. It was from this milieu that the new emphasis on individual rights sprang. The impetus grew as the misery inflicted on laborers and their families during the Industrial Revolution became evident. Persons who moved to the cities to take jobs in factories were often left to their own devices. Whatever social contract might have been in force in earlier days was well on the way to dissolving by that time. With the disruption in society and the gradual weakening of the family, with the increased social mobility brought on by economic growth, the individual had to be positioned to take care of himself or herself.

Where individualism reigns, then, the stage is set for individual human rights. Where economic development brings dislocation and alienation of persons, the appeal to such rights becomes imperative. Island societies, partially transformed by modernization in recent years, are on this same path. As the extended family is being reshaped by the cash economy, the status of the individual has been elevated in recent years. The individual Micronesian today enjoys a much larger personal sphere than he or she would have forty years ago. The person has more privacy, more personal choice, greater claim to private property, and a stronger sense of individuality. We can assume that in due time rights theory, like MTV and western dress styles and the computer, will become an established part of life even in the islands of Micronesia. This could happen in ten years, or in thirty years, or in fifty years. Yet, the cultural chasm has not yet been crossed in most of Micronesia. This should come as no surprise because the transition from the old social order to a new stress on individual rights took centuries to accomplish in the West.

Rights language is still not fully understood or accepted in Micronesia, just as it is not in many other parts of the world. There was no word for "rights" in the indigenous language of most island peoples. The word itself sometimes draws jeers from older people, who speak of "rights" as a kind of disease afflicting the young. The very term "rights," in the minds of many older islanders, stands for a selfish individualism and all its attendant evils. It is tantamount to embracing the cause of the single human person over and against the good of the entire society, selfishness versus communitarianism. In the minds of many, the modern advocacy of rights is one of the most pernicious contagions that the West has unleashed on traditional and proud societies: the misguided emphasis on "me" rather than "us."

The people of Chuuk, an island group on which I worked for twenty-five years, used to speak with disdain of a philosophy that emphasized what one is entitled to receive (rights) instead of what one is obligated to give (responsibilities). They saw this as puerile and simply pandering to the silly tastes of the young, who were always trying to get a better deal for themselves. In their minds, a code of social justice that was built on rights ran the risk of condoning irresponsibility.

A further criticism of rights theory heard in Micronesia is that it is confrontational rather than conciliatory, reflecting western legal tradition as it does. The rights of one person, after all, are bound to clash with those of another, resulting in adversarial positions that must be adjudicated. In other words, rights theory more often generates an open confrontation rather than the kind of consensus Pacific island societies characteristically try to achieve. The island alternative to this is making known various parties' needs and trying to meet these through consensus.

Overall, the critique of individual rights I hear from many Micronesians is that the concept is rooted in radical individualism, self-seeking rather than giving, and confrontational rather than consensual. For this reason, rights language is often perceived as inimical to the Micronesian way. To champion the individual rights of members of a social group was to risk turning the community into a social battleground, and no one wanted that.

Micronesian folklore is filled with cautionary tales told to children to warn them of the dangers of individual pride and the fragmentation it might cause. The assumption of islanders has always been that if they looked to the common good of the group, the group would, in turn, take care of them. The best assurance of protection was to turn to the family and depend on their support in time of trouble. "Family first, and we all win" is the way many people might put it.

As long as the Micronesian today recognizes the strong claims of the family on him, his commitment to individual rights will be half-hearted at best. Only when the social identity gives way to the radical individualism of the West will the protection that human rights afford be fully embraced by the islands. But as this happens, islanders will also have to struggle with the negative effects of the breakdown of the social identity. The change might well be inevitable. But when it comes, it may prove as painful as beneficial to islanders.

«•«•« 4 »•»•»

The Place of Wealth

Food in Abundance

We took our seats at the table outside the church amid a flurry of activity. The three-hour liturgy at which two men had been ordained pastors in the Protestant church had concluded with blessings from several of the clergy in attendance, including me, a Catholic priest. Now the visiting pastors were doffing their suit coats and loosening their ties as they seated themselves for the lunch that was to follow the ordination. Women moved back and forth around the table making sure that everyone was in his proper place and that the food was laid out properly.

In front of me, as I sat down, was a very large plastic basin over-flowing with food of all kinds: a five-pound bag of sugar, a large bottle of soy sauce, cans of sardines and meat, packages of cookies, a whole broiled chicken in Saran Wrap, a bag containing a dozen fresh rolls, two plastic bottles of soda, and a number of other items. I looked with amazement at the container and started to rummage through it looking for something to eat. One of the women serving us stopped me and asked if perhaps I would like a sandwich to eat or perhaps a little sliced breadfruit. I picked up a tuna fish sandwich and had just started eating it when the men around me began rising from the table. Lunch was finished, barely fifteen minutes after we had seated ourselves.

I stood to leave and went to the head of the table to thank our hosts. As I did, one of the women instructed me to wait until she got one of the young men to carry my fifty-pound bag of rice to my car. So three of us headed to the car—myself with a half-eaten sandwich in hand, a boy carrying the basin of foodstuffs that had been at my place at table, and another young man hauling the bag of rice.

Micronesian generosity is legendary. Any visitor to the islands can recount tales of island largesse: attending parties and being provided with much more food than he could possibly eat, sometimes being sent off with enough to feed his family for a week. We old-timers in Chuuk always chuckled when a host announced, with typical island modesty, that he had not prepared much for his guests, just "a little bread and some water." We knew by that time what to expect as platter after platter of food was brought out along with an assortment of drinks. The eyes of the newcomers among us would widen as they began to realize that what they expected to be a modest repast was in fact a sumptuous feast. But just in case some of the guests were not able to eat the breadfruit and taro and fish served as the main course, there was also broiled chicken, sandwiches, and cookies.

Food has always held a central place in island culture. "Come and eat" or "Have you eaten?" was once the standard greeting to a passerby in place of a hello. It was an invitation to stop by and share food with the people of that household. When a family was undergoing hardship of any sort, especially when they had lost someone to death, neighbors responded by showing their concern in the form of food gifts to the family. Food gifts were a gesture of support to those in distress; they were an assurance of solidarity when shared within the family; they were everywhere a sign of care and a token of love. To provide food for someone was to nourish that person, to show that you valued that person highly. To share food with another household was to strengthen and seal the bond of affection between your family and that household.

In Micronesia it was the shared food itself, not the act of eating together, that was significant as a bonding element. The food might simply be wrapped and presented to the recipients to be used when and how they wanted. Generally, the sharing of food in the islands did not take the form of the conviviality of an Italian family enjoying a meal that may last all Sunday afternoon, bubbling with conversation the whole time. Families rarely ate together as family groups, and when they did they usually did not intersperse conversation with eating. As the late Fr. Felix Yaoch often recalled, Palauans used to chide children who were loquacious at mealtime: "Do you have two mouths so that you can eat and talk at the same time?"

If furnishing food held such meaning in island culture, the denial of food was also an important statement. If food was a symbol of nurturing love, then refusing food or its surrogates to another could be understood as withholding love from that person. This understanding seems to underlie many of the youth suicides that occur in Micronesia today, as it did the suicide of the young man described in Chapter 2. A young man who is refused something—more often money or material items than food—takes this refusal as a lack of interest in him. It is not the denial of the object he is requesting, but the lack of concern for him personally that pushes him to end his relationship with his family. The pattern of contemporary suicides and their motives are strong evidence that the relationship between "food" in its different forms and "love" is as strong today as ever.

The strong association between "food" and "love" may also explain the embarrassment Micronesians feel at not providing enough for a guest. To send a guest away hungry was regarded as a terrible thing: something akin to a sin against hospitality. To avoid this, people would use the last bit of food in their house and then, if necessary, go into debt to buy what was needed to satisfy a guest. In Chuuk, as in probably most other island cultures, "stingy" was one of the worst adjectives that could be used to describe a person. Time and again I've seen a smoker offer his last cigarette to someone who had none. I admired the patience of people who never seemed to refuse cigarettes, food, or anything to those who habitually cadged from others. Islanders eating out together in a restaurant would quickly pick up the check, practically fight for it if they had to, rather than start calculating who ate what so as to divide up the tab, as westerners sometimes do. Better be taken advantage of many times over than run the risk of incurring the reputation of being stingy.

So important was generosity in the island hierarchy of values that the exercise of it could become a contest. Competitive feasting was a recognized cultural feature in Chuuk and Yap, where one village would invite another for a party while the other would later reciprocate. The point of the contest was to outdo the rival in generosity. In other words, one wins by producing more food, surrendering more material resources than the other. The tradition continues up to the present, although in a slightly different context. Churches may compete with one another to provide the most food at a celebration like the one described above. If one church presents each of the guests with a large basin of food and a fifty-pound sack of rice, the next church to stage an event will most likely up the amount, if only to avoid being outdone. This competitive instinct also is evident outside the church; island groups try to outdo each other in the lavishness of the receptions given at official events that rotate from one place to another. Competitive feasting survives in many forms even today.

The lavish presentation of food and other resources to chiefs was a customary means of gaining prestige on some islands. On Pohnpei gifts of pigs, yams, and *sakau* (kava) were offered on special occasions, and in Yap and Palau taro served the same purpose. The size of the gift was thought to be a measure of the generosity of the contributing individual or family, and this in turn elevated their status in the community. Even today those Micronesian families that still work the land take much greater pains in cultivating the produce that will be offered as gifts at community events than the food they themselves will consume.

In the West prestige may be derived from the mere possession of resources—money, buildings, sports cars, private planes—for they are testimony to the skill and energy of the one who was able to accumulate such wealth. In traditional Micronesia, however, accumulated wealth meant nothing. It was the surrender of this wealth to build up or strengthen interpersonal relationships that counted for everything.

Investing in People

The middle-aged American man had just come home from work and settled himself in the living room to read the paper when his Palauan wife sat down in a chair next to him. She started her recital of everything that had happened that day, adding, almost as an afterthought, that she had just heard that one of her uncles had passed away in Palau. He was old and had been housebound with illness for more than a year, she told her husband, so his death came as no great surprise to anyone in the family. Her husband waited silently for what he knew was to come next.

"We should send the family a contribution for the funeral," his wife reminded him. "Can we make out a check for $3,000?"

"What about $1,500?" he suggested. "We have a lot of other bills that have to be paid this month. And then there's our daughter's college tuition that is due. All that is going to take a big bite out of our savings."

"Didn't you hear what I just said?" was his wife's rejoinder. "The family is expecting a contribution of $3,000 from us. You do remember that they were the ones who took care of us when we visited Palau a few years ago, don't you? Besides, I was always very close to them when I was still a young girl."

Her husband paused to let this soak in before he made one last attempt to compromise. "You're right. We really should do something for them, but why can't we give them $1,500 now and offer them more help later when we're in better shape financially?"

Fig. 5. **Chuukese at a church feast (ca. 1970).** Courtesy of Craig Severance.

*"Don't you remember that old Palauan saying that I taught
you years ago? Have you forgotten what it means to us islanders? 'What I gave I have. What I spent I had. What I kept I lost.'
Well, this is our chance to give rather than keep," she said.*

My first impression of people in the islands was that Micronesians
appeared ready to surrender food reserves, household goods, even the
family boat or car, almost anything at all for the sake of personal
relationships. Admittedly, I used to wonder whether it was just their
own innate generosity or a desire for status in the eyes of the community that prompted such open-handedness. I knew that islanders,
like all of us, kept a sharp eye out for the way others in their society
regarded them, but I couldn't believe that pure self-interest was the
motive. Whatever the case, the old Palauan saying that the wife cited
in the vignette above seemed to encapsulate perfectly people's thinking: Why keep what you have acquired when you have the chance to
give it away?

It wasn't just the lavish gifts of food at feasts or the farewell gifts
people would heap on someone who was leaving island. They were
also cavalier about reclaiming goods that they had lent to others.
Whatever they gave to another—whether an outboard engine, a sew-
ing machine, or a cell phone—seemed to be given in an open-ended
fashion with the full knowledge that they might never get the object
back again. We all found out through experience that the same applied
to "loans" of money. "Micronesian borrowing," as we called it, might
drive Americans crazy but it never seemed to bother islanders. At least,
they never admitted that it did.

"Giving rather than keeping," as the Palauan woman put it, makes
sense in a society in which personal relationships are more valued than
material wealth. Personal ties were the heart and soul of any island
society; they were the means of survival and satisfaction. Personal
ties endured and even strengthened over time, while material possessions were merely transient. The accumulation of material things
didn't make any sense in a traditional island society: food rotted, so
did canoes and buildings made of wood, and the material for producing these objects was available to just about everyone. It was only
when foreign traders began to offer materials from the outside—iron
pots, cotton and gingham dresses, metal tools—that stockpiling mate-

rial goods became a viable option. But even then, the strong cultural preference for sharing rather than keeping acted as a real inhibition against trading for these items and hiding them away somewhere for one's own use.

Although Micronesians wouldn't have used the expression, they were converting material goods into social capital. Another way of putting it is that they were investing in people. In giving away much of their wealth, islanders were just doing what came naturally to them from a cultural point of view. The use of resources to help others in need was a strong part of the social code everywhere in Micronesia. From a pragmatic point of view, however, they were providing assistance to others in the community, who in turn would feel obligated to help them when need arose in the future. Reciprocity was a strong feature in island society: one gift was sure to be repaid by another of equal or greater value. Their gifts, then, built up strong relationships throughout the community even as they served as insurance against the setbacks they might face in the days and years ahead.

Just as food and island produce was converted into social capital in the past, money might be used for that purpose today. Indeed, some of the financial decisions that are made by island business-men—decisions that baffle western economists and business advis-ers—only make sense when viewed from this perspective. Some years ago, the anthropologist Glenn Petersen published an article explaining why mom-and-pop stores on Pohnpei sprouted up all over the island despite the fact that the life span of the typical small store in a Pohn-peian village was less than a year. Why would villagers who had saved a little money set up a small store that was almost certainly doomed to failure? Petersen explained that the owners might lose the $5,000 or so they invested in stock, but they would hold chits from those people who had taken what they needed on credit that had never been repaid. All this meant that whatever financial losses they had sustained, the owners had gained considerable social capital—namely, the sense of obligation that those who never repaid their loans felt toward them. This and the respect that they acquired from the community as gener-ous people was more than enough to compensate them for their busi-ness failure.

Unpaid loans of any kind, money given prodigally to people in need, financial assistance of any sort—all bring the same rewards to the people who bestow them. Neither business decisions nor family finances—nor, in fact, the entire island economy—can be understood unless this principle is taken into account. Goods and money can be converted into social capital—and this is the preferred form of investment in a society in which personal and social relationships count for so much. In the end, these relationships will trump the mere accumulation of what westerners count as wealth.

This mind-set helps explain much more in island life. The attitude toward children, for example, can be viewed as an extension of the preference for social capital. Why would a family that already has six children count four or five more as a blessing rather than as a liability? That is, in fact, how traditional island families would have regarded a large family. Children are loved and cherished in their own right, of course, but they are also regarded as a kind of investment—a form of social security for parents that was preferable to a pension plan or a healthy bank account. When the children married, they would acquire a network of social relationships that would expand those that the parents already had. Or if they married cousins or close relatives, as was often the case in the past, they would strengthen existing bonds within the larger family. But they would also be expected to take care of their parents in their old age. If some of the children later moved off island to live abroad, there were others who could be expected to fill this role. All this explains why many children were preferred to few.

Couples who were childless would often adopt the child of a relative to rear. This would provide the same benefits: it would strengthen the ties with the natural parents of the adopted child, while aiding the childless couple in the future. How could a Micronesian couple not afford to raise children when the kids would provide for their parents when they became old? The western calculus, on the other hand, is very different: How can parents afford to have a third or fourth child when this will mean money spent for clothes, education, and upkeep? Furthermore, there is no expectation in the West that children will care for parents later on except in the case of dire necessity; parents depend on their own savings to support themselves in old age.

The island penchant for investing in people, rooted in the importance placed on personal relationships in island societies, explains much of how resources from the land and sea have always been

Fig. 6. Marshallese woman and children at a roadside store (ca. 1980).
Courtesy of Giff Johnson.

utilized, how money is so often used today, and how islanders have regarded children. It is the key to understanding the island attitude toward wealth and how it is to be used.

Coping with the Cash Economy

Lorenzo stood at the office door, shifting from foot to foot as he waited to see his boss. Finally his boss looked up from the pile of papers on his desk and invited him into the office. Lorenzo scratched his head, stared at the floor for a moment, and then blurted out his request. He asked his boss for a loan of $80, requesting that the money be added to his paycheck the next day. When his boss wanted to know what the loan was for, Lorenzo told him that his wife's brother had just died and that he and his family were expected to contribute to the expense of the funeral.

The boss narrowed his eyes and reminded Lorenzo that he still owed $120 from his previous loans. Lorenzo look bewildered

for a split second before he replied, "Oh, that was the money I
borrowed for the birthday party for our one-year-old child."

"Look, Lorenzo," the boss said, "you've been asking for
loans nearly every month this year. First it was the trip your uncle
was making to Guam, then it was the hospital bill for someone
in your family, and then something else. When are you going to
stop asking for loans? Maybe you need to put away a little money
each week to save up for emergencies like these. Why don't you
set up a little account so that you don't have to keep coming in
for loans all the time."

The shift to the cash economy that has accelerated in the last several years has created new problems. Before contact with the West and
imported trade goods, as we have noted, it would have been pointless
to accumulate wealth because foodstuffs eventually spoiled anyway.
Besides, everyone had access to the same food and the same material
goods, so why bother to accumulate anything? It was more sensible
to share the fish you had caught with a number of other people in the
understanding that they would do the same for you when they had a
large catch. Reciprocity was honored, and so food could be shared
without doing damage to your family. In giving a portion of your
catch to others on the island, you were creating not just goodwill, but
obligations on the part of others. If, someday, you were without any
protein, you might hope to receive fish from someone else.

With the coming of western goods—canned meat, fabrics, and a
variety of electronic products in our own day—there is an alternative
to disposing of wealth by distributing what you can't consume yourself. You can save it, stockpile it, and exchange it for other imported
goods that you don't have. Or you can convert it into cash, so that
you can buy something with it later. Money can be stashed away, converted into any type of material good, and used for the same prestige
purposes for which food had once been used. Besides, money can be
earned by the individual; it does not necessarily depend on the efforts
of the extended family, as food crops and building materials would
have.

Even in the past, it should be noted, there were possessions that
belonged solely to the individual, although these did not include
money. Objects of special importance to the person—items of cloth-

ing, ornamental belts made of shell, or special keepsakes—might be kept in a locked trunk in the house or tucked away up on the rafters of the residence. In some island societies small canoes might be personally owned. On all islands there were personal possessions that could be disposed of at the owner's will, even if they could not be converted into just about anything else, as money could.

Money is a game-changer. Not only can it be used to purchase just about anything, but it is earned for the most part by an individual with a salary in private business or a government job. A cash economy, then, is tailor-made for the individual and his needs. Yet, a Micronesian who has a regular salary still has a network of relationships through his family, and obligations to the many people socially linked to him. He may live in a time of individual liberation, at least from a purely economic standpoint, but he remains as much a social animal as ever.

As long as a Micronesian retains the thick web of important personal relationships centered in the extended family, he will be called on to come to the aid of these people as needs arise. The calls for help are bound to occur more frequently today than ever before, if only because modernization multiplies the opportunities for assistance. A seriously sick relative who once might have been sent home to await the end now has the option of referral to a hospital overseas for treatment. But wage earners in the family will be asked to commit a substantial amount of money to help the family pay for the airline tickets to get him and his attendant off island. A young nephew with a bright academic future might be accepted into a private high school or college, but the family will need help in paying his tuition and boarding fees. Someone in the family would like to purchase a used car from Japan, but he doesn't have the money to cover the purchase. Accordingly, he turns to his extended family for the support that he has come to expect from them. In Palau at one time the lineage would turn to its members and others in its social network for assistance in building its lineage house. In the past this meant donations of labor and local materials. Today, however, the traditional custom (*ocheraol*) has come to be applied to the construction of expensive modern homes and business offices, and even extended to costly boats and cars. The social network is still tagged for contributions, with the assessment for each family member sometimes running up to several thousand dollars.

Hence, the islander today finds himself in a quandary. His social network remains as broad as ever, while the cost of fulfilling these multiple obligations has risen sharply. He must try to respond to the needs of those in his broad social network, centered on his extended family, while providing for his own household out of the limited resources he has available to him. This requires a delicate balance and a great deal of diplomacy; it is a challenging situation with potential for financial disaster.

Under conditions like these, people with any resources at their disposal will be tempted to use them to meet immediate family needs. A businessman who should know better may find himself digging into his company resources in order to provide for a family emergency. In doing so, he is acutely aware that he will incur the displeasure of his foreign advisers for failing to cordon off his business assets from his family finances. They will remind him that bad business practices often arise from just such situations. Lapses of this sort lead to business failures and are sometimes blamed for the stunted growth of the private sector in Micronesia. Yet, more often than not these practices stem from the conflict between a person's need to preserve his wealth and his commitment to his family. It's not hard to guess which usually wins out.

One doesn't have to be a businessman to face such conflicts. Any wage earner who has money in the bank will have to decide whether he should withdraw the money needed to meet the request for help or maintain a sufficient balance to see his own household through its own needs. Here the decision is not between care for his business and care for his family, but between family and family—his extended family and his immediate family.

Lorenzo, in the vignette that began this section, illustrates the way in which many Micronesians are now coping with this dilemma. Against the advice of his boss, who recommends that Lorenzo start to put away some of his money in a savings account to deal with emergencies, he continues to ask for loans and advances to provide for unforeseen family needs. He knows that any money he puts in a savings account would soon be gobbled up by the family, for he would be called on to share generously with his relatives whatever was in the account and more. Instead, he adopts the strategy of the zero-balance budget, deliberately spending everything he makes. He honors the age-old practice of putting at the disposal of the extended family his resources, but he also recognizes the need for a control on his generosity in the day of the cash economy. The zero-balance budget puts a limit on the money that can be used for family support—a limit imposed by what he can borrow (from the bank or his employer) and repay in a reasonable length of time.

There may be other ways of striking a compromise between the needs of one's immediate family and obligations to the extended family, but this appears to be one of the most common. Yet it runs counter to the conventional wisdom of the West: tuck some money away for a rainy day. It also is at odds with the prevailing western counsel on the importance of saving with an eye to investment. Even so, it is a sensible strategy for islanders with a modest income who are determined to continue to invest, as they always have, in their family and their social network.

« · « · « 5 » · » · »

The Uses of Information

Watching One's Words

I was in the airport lounge on Guam talking to a Chuukese man about a suicide in his family. He had recognized me and had come over to say hello, and in the course of our conversation he had mentioned the suicide of his son. I was a bit surprised at his willingness to talk about such a personal issue, something that I rarely encountered in dealings with people anywhere in Micronesia. He knew that I was a priest, of course, and was asking for prayers for his family during this difficult time, but he also knew that I had been studying suicide for many years. As we chatted about the death, he seemed to have little hesitation in discussing the more intimate details of the tragedy. At one point in our conversation, however, I mentioned to him a little of what I had already learned about his son's relationship with some of those in his family. At this, he paused for a moment and asked me a single question: Who had told me all this?

I was not terribly taken aback by the question because during the years I had been dealing with sensitive issues I had heard that same question again and again. My experience had taught me that any time I offered any new information that might reflect back on the family, or ventured a possible explanation of the death, the person with whom I was talking would not contradict or expand on the explanation. Instead, he would ask where I had obtained the information. It seemed to me that the reliability of the information I was offering was secondary. The dominant concern was to find out who had said what to me about the matter.

Facts are just facts, we westerners would like to believe. Our concern is to know whether the facts are correct or not so that we can construct as accurate a description of the event as possible. Is it true in the situation described above, for instance, that the son had begun drinking heavily a few months before his death, possibly because of some misunderstanding in the family? Was the son angry at someone in his family for a particular reason? My informant, however, had a different agenda. He wanted to know the source of the stories I had been told. The main issue for him was not the reliability of what I had been told, but who had revealed the information to me. If he knew the source, he might be able to form conclusions of his own about the intention of the person who had been talking to me. For one thing, he could make inferences on how well disposed the informant was to his family. Information can be filtered of personal biases to piece together an objective account, or it can be processed in such a way as to expose those very biases. Is it so surprising that Micronesians should have a distinct preference for the latter? After all, everything in a small island society comes back to personal relations in the end.

If wealth and food serve the higher end of fostering interpersonal relations, so does information. Oddly enough, at least from a western point of view, Micronesians appear almost wantonly generous with wealth but extraordinarily guarded in dispensing information. This paradox can be traced back to the same foundational island value—the importance of preserving social relations. Island societies are person-oriented, as we have repeatedly seen, and so a great deal of cultural practice reflects this basic orientation. Again and again this fundamental value surfaces in the different areas explored in this book. To be sure, information in its own right was a precious commodity in traditional times and was not dispensed carelessly. But information could also be dangerous insofar as it might hurt someone and cause a break in a personal relationship. Hence, it was doubly sacred and had to be meted out with great care.

In my experience, islanders are very slow to say anything that might reflect badly on a third party, even in personal conversation. Part of the hesitation may stem from deference to the feelings of the person they are addressing. You can never be entirely certain, even in tight-knit island societies, whether the person you're talking about is a friend or foe of your conversation partner. But another large part of the reluctance is owing to the fact that personal relationships are easily damaged in a small island community. Understandably, no one wants to say anything negative that could get back to the person and create ill will. It's one thing to take that chance in a large American city, but quite another to risk such enmity in a small society that virtually guarantees personal encounters on a day-to-day basis.

Tracing information back to the source has been developed to a fine art in the islands. Many of us have had the experience of having made offhand remarks about a situation only to find, some weeks or days later, that our remarks, along with the attribution to us, have made their way to one of the persons involved. In private conversation with someone, I once deplored the disorganization of an institution on another island. Three weeks later I was confronted by the chief administrator of the organization, who demanded to know why I was badmouthing him. The personal confrontation was atypical in the islands—normally word would have come back to me indirectly, through a third party, that he was offended by my slight of his management—but the speed with which he learned of my remark was not. Word travels quickly through the islands by route of what we all call the "coconut wireless." Anyone who wants to keep the peace and maintain his friends, however outspoken he might be, learns sooner or later to watch his words.

The fear of indiscretion in speech has other ramifications. Some years ago a congressman, smarting at the accusation that FSM Congress pork barrel funds were being misused, presented me with an interesting challenge. He asked me to check on his own special projects money over the past five years to verify that the money had been spent legitimately on the projects for which they were designated. Since I had publicly questioned the use of these funds on several occasions, my interest in this project was as great as the congressman's. Both of us stood to learn something useful from the project. I immediately sent out an older American with time on his hands who had volunteered his help to obtain the information we needed. Armed with a list of projects funded, he spent a month visiting offices and talking to officials. When he returned at the end of the month to report on what he had accomplished, he was frustrated and seemed defeated. The government officials he visited weren't rude to him, but they were clearly reluctant to release the information he needed for our little study. "Why do you want to know this?" was the most common response he encountered. The long delays and the endless chase from one office to another were as effective as if doors had been slammed shut. In the end, we had to abandon our project to the dismay of both the congressman and myself. We had been defeated by the unwillingness of government functionaries to release the information we needed, all because they were afraid that it could be used to damage someone.

Even if no malice was intended, the information could be misinterpreted by those who gained access to it, reflecting badly on the congressman. Worse still, its release could be traced back to the one who surrendered the information, with damaging effects for this individual and his job. I'm sure that this was why my colleague, who went from office to office seeking information on congressional funds, was met so often by the question: "Why do you need this information?"

This is just the sort of barrier that so many of us hit when we try to gather "public" information on a government issue. Sometimes we are told that the computer is down. We may be told to wait until the office supervisor returns so that he can authorize the release of the information we need. To protest that what we seek is "public information" is of little avail. In practice, public information is a rare commodity in Micronesia today. Even when there is nothing to hide, people seem reluctant to share information. This often confounds westerners because the same islanders who are so generous with food and material things can be astonishingly withholding of their knowledge.

The Right to Know

Our discussion on freedom of the press had just begun when one of the participants gave a rousing little talk in favor of a free press in the islands. "It's the press," he remarked, "that holds public officials accountable in the United States and keeps them relatively honest out of the fear that they will be caught in their wrongdoing. If the islands had vigorous press reporting, public officials would think long and hard before they took advantage of their position to bully people or use public funds on themselves."

Someone objected: "But it's against our culture to publish nasty things about people, even when they're true. We Microne-

*sians just can't name names publicly, whether in our conversation
or in a newspaper."*

*"That's true," another participant said. "But in our modern
age new institutions are needed to do what traditional means
could handle in simpler times. A new age brings new problems,
and that means new solutions. If we want democracy to work,
we'd better be ready to adopt whatever we need to protect it."*

*"That's going to require a huge change in thinking," someone
objected. "People are going to be angry; this new approach is
going to provoke fights, maybe even deaths."*

*Someone else recounted how he happened to be on Guam
when the Freedom of Information Act was put into effect there.
Some of the early newspaper articles provoked outcries and
resulted in lawsuits, but in time the people of Guam got used
to the press' hard-hitting approach. "If they did it, we can,"
he concluded.*

The establishment of the media with its roving band of news
hawks has made government officials all the more wary of releasing
information to the public. While most island governments appreciate
the need to issue press releases on newsworthy events, they are much
more reluctant to offer the unedited facts to newspapers and other
media outlets for fear that the media will put an unfavorable spin on
the information. Pacific Island governments, in their desire to control
the release of information, do not easily embrace the idea of others
gleaning what they can to present their own interpretation of events.
A congressman from the Marshall Islands once complained: "Some
people access government information and distort the truth to mislead
people." He added that, while he believes in transparency in government, "Something needs to be done to safeguard information so that
not just anyone can access it."

The position he was reflecting is a common one in Micronesian
government circles: the danger of twisting information so as to misrepresent the government is serious enough to justify withholding such
information altogether. The danger, of course, is compounded in an
age in which new channels of communication carry messages instantaneously to large numbers of people. Thus, the perceived threat of
damage that information can cause has expanded—from damage to

the individual to damage to the government itself. The desire to maintain a decent public face is surely important to all governments, but to
none so much as island governments.

On the other hand, modern standards of good governance demand
a transparency that is at odds with this guardedness toward information. Unless people know what the government is doing, the theory
goes, there will never be any public accountability. Hence, the government is obliged to lift the veil that conceals its inner workings so that
citizens can peek in, if they care to, and find out what is happening in
the government. To the extent that the government removes the barri-
cades at the door, throws open its windows, and provides information
to its citizens, it can be said to practice transparency in government—a
phrase that has become a catchphrase in our day.

Media not only offers the means to convey this information to
the public—at least in most societies—but it also represents a group
of dedicated information seekers who will stubbornly pursue officials
who don't return their calls and will keep knocking on doors that are
slow to open. It has the resources and interest, despite the delays and
rebuffs from officials, to convey to the rest of us what's going on in
government. Theoretically, then, media is a critical element in ensuring
good governance in that it provides a steady flow of reliable information from government offices to the public. Without such information
the public would never be able to make an informed judgment on
the performance of their leaders. If the media functions as it should,
people will supposedly act on this information and vote corrupt or
ineffective leaders out of office and replace them with a better lot.

Herein lies the conflict, however. Government functionaries more
often than not understand their job as protecting their leaders from
any harm. This, after all, is the default mode for handling information
in an island society. On the other hand, those working for the media
view the release of such information as indispensable for the public in
a modern society. Ordinary people, who are entrusted with the final
responsibility for the workings of their government, have a "right to
know," they insist.

Battles lines are drawn even more sharply because of the differing
interpretations of the "right to know." There is a shared understanding in Micronesia that some things, even facts known by everyone,
should not be discussed publicly. The paternity of an important public

official, for instance, or his sexual preferences or past indiscretions might be generally acknowledged, even though it is tacitly understood that they are not to be mentioned. Yet, some of the champions of a very free press are seen as challenging this pact by their assertion: "If it's news, then the people have a right to hear about it, even in a public forum." One westerner who edited a monthly paper in Micronesia some years ago, in her insistence in following this principle, published personal information on certain leaders that astonished even the expatriates on the island. After a protracted debate on how far the limits of tolerance should be extended to the media, she was declared a persona non grata and barred from returning to the islands.

The press may be the watchdog over society, as westerners insist, but does this mean that it may disregard all the norms that once governed island societies? Should the press not only be allowed to point out questionable practices in government, but also list the names of those officials who have abused their public trust? If so, what will become of the respect to which all people, even miscreants, were enti-

Fig. 7. Residents in the Marshalls reading the weekly newspaper (ca. 1980).
Courtesy of Giff Johnson.

tled in traditional society? Although a free press may intend to pursue issues and check abuses rather than target individuals, it rarely is able to do so without naming persons.

Some participants in the discussion cited above felt that a dishonest official forfeits any right to respect and merits the embarrassment that results from full disclosure of his wrongdoing. Others maintained the opposite: no one forfeits respect in island culture, no matter how great and numerous his misdeeds. This is precisely the difference between Micronesian and American culture, they argued. In Micronesian societies mutual respect acts as the bonding agent; it is, one islander suggested, what keeps people from one another's throats and what prevents society from falling into "barbarism."

The discussion of whether traditional norms should be superseded by modern ones continues as the "right to know" is debated in the islands today. Some argue, like the discussants in the opening vignette, that modern institutions are needed to do today what the old institutions could handle in simpler times. A new age brings new problems that demand new solutions, however much our respect for tradition. If we want the democracy that is so integral to life in the modern world, we must also adopt the means that are necessary to protect it. This will demand island people's readiness to make real changes. The press and other media may not always be gentle in their methods, but they can be highly effective.

Others maintain that media must be subject to at least the most basic cultural restraints that have long held force in the islands. If the press is to be at all sensitive to Micronesian culture, it cannot afford to be as open and direct as its western counterpart. In reply to those who insist that the unsparing honesty of modern media is necessary if corrupt leaders are to be kept in check, one person likened the press to a knife. In the hands of a skilled surgeon it can heal, but in the hands of another the knife can become a weapon.

Even as the debate continues, most island people clearly show a strong gut dislike of public criticism in any form. When, a few years ago, I went public with my article on the problems that the Chuuk government was experiencing, many persons wrote in to object, some of them quite angrily, to what they considered an assault on the reputation of Chuuk. "Why would anyone want to hang out their dirty laundry in public?" one of them asked. I could protest that the laundry was already on the line before I got there, or that the purpose of the article was not to vilify Chuuk, and certainly not to smear the reputation of any individuals, but simply to get people thinking and talking about how they could best deal with what were undeniably their problems.

I was the typical westerner in my insistence that such public criticism was the best way to ensure better performance by public officials. Yet, I have to admit that the reluctance to criticize openly is one of the many qualities that I find endearing in the Pacific. I regard the desire to spare the feelings of others as admirable. Well I should, because I myself have profited from this forgivingness many times over. But the issue is not whether the attitude is noble—that is taken for granted—but at what point it must give way to another, more demanding approach in a modern government system. How do we get a government to work properly if everyone is forgiven everything and not a word of criticism is ever heard in public?

As with so many other modern values, the "right to know" is a disputed issue, if only because it is so antithetical to old island values. Yet, it is presented today as one of the essential components in a modern island nation to ensure good governance. Micronesians will have to decide for themselves just how far they want to allow the media to go. They have it within their power to determine whether the "watchdog" will be a pit bull or a collie, as one islander put it. But they will also have to accept the consequences of their decision.

The Value of Information

The man staggered under the burden of a heavy sack of rice as he struggled up the slope on his way to Osiro's house. Osiro, now an old man in frail health, was one of the most respected men on the island. He was reputed to have learned Japanese and even some German, although his knowledge of English was limited. But he was best known for his broad knowledge of the old cultural ways. He was reputed to be an expert in local medicine and healing techniques as well as in local history. People who had visited him attested that he had an encyclopedic knowledge of the history of land parcels in his area, with the ability to recount details that had long been forgotten by most people.

As the man reached Osiro's house, he stopped in respect-
ful silence for a moment before he called out a greeting to those
inside. He was invited in, still carrying the sack of rice, as Osiro
appeared before him. After bowing respectfully, the man placed
the sack of rice on the floor and proceeded to speak: "As heavy
as this burden is, it is light compared to the burden of my debt to
you and your family for your help. Sir, we ask your help to assist
our family in our struggles and woes."

The man then gestured at the sack of rice, apologized that it
was well below the value of what he was seeking from Osiro, and
then asked him in a long and indirect fashion to provide some
details on the history of a piece of land that was claimed by his
family but was being contested by another.

In a society without books and libraries, the only way valuable
information could be stored was inside the heads of those who possessed it, and this information was not dispensed lightly. In island societies a treasury of such information resided in certain persons, each of
whom possessed particular factual knowledge that could be accessed
only by contract with the individual under carefully regulated conditions. Osiro, for instance, was a local historian who knew the history
of landholdings in his part of the island. This information was of considerable importance to others in his community, especially landowners who needed what he knew to support their claim to a piece of land.
Osiro would certainly have provided this knowledge freely to his own
family or to others within his close social network. If anyone outside
that circle had a need for this information, he would have to pay for
it, as the supplicant with the sack of rice did.

Old island societies had their recognized experts in many different
areas. Healing was one of the most important and sought-after services, with specialists in various types of medicine. There were persons
who were skilled in the art of massage, while others were called on to
provide herbal medicines for various maladies. Since many diseases
were attributed to the influence of sorcery or evil spirits, other specialists were sought to diagnose the cause of the illness and to employ
spiritual remedies to counter the curse or sorcery. Still others were
called on to communicate directly with the patron spirits of their community to find answers for these or other questions. In Palau, certain

persons known to be particularly susceptible to being possessed by spirits were frequently asked for help in consulting the patron spirit of the place. In return for this, they received gifts and achieved a status that came to rival that of the district chiefs.

There were also other types of experts. In the coral atolls, where long-distance voyages were regularly made until recently, the master craftsman who supervised the construction of the large canoes used for these voyages was given special recognition. According to island thinking, the skills he possessed were not simply the result of long experience in his trade, but the product of instruction from others before him and sometimes from the deities. Hence, he was regarded as blessed with privileged information that allowed him to exercise his craft in a superior manner. Celestial navigation over the open sea was another special skill, one that required long apprenticeship under a master navigator. In some islands there were different schools of navigation, each headed by an older man who had attained a reputation as a respected senior navigator.

In each of these areas there were what we would call professionals. They may have acquired their mastery by sitting at the feet of an older person who was a recognized expert. Often the information and skills associated with the area of specialization were passed down from someone in his own lineage, almost as a family heirloom. He, in turn, might be expected to pass it on to one of his own younger relatives when the time came. Sometimes the expert might take on an apprentice outside his family circle, but if he did so he would expect to be well compensated for the information he passed along. The traditional expert did not offer his services gratis any more than a lawyer or doctor would do so today. Food might be freely shared in the islands, but not specialized information. Indeed, this type of information conferred not only prestige on the one possessing it, but a measure of wealth as well.

Even today specialized information is often seen as the valued possession of those fortunate enough to be in the know. This type of knowledge can still be parlayed into personal prestige.

It frequently happens that a person working for the government, or even for a private organization, will be invited to a conference or workshop designed to impart information that might be helpful in confronting critical problems. A person working in health services, for instance, could be asked to attend an international gathering to update governments on recently discovered types of hepatitis or a new epidemic that threatens island populations. An educator might be invited to a gathering to discuss recent findings on different approaches to literacy. The invitations are offered with the expectation that this knowledge will be circulated among the staff when the representative returns home. Yet, the purpose of the conference in the eyes of the convenors is more often than not frustrated when islanders return and resume work without breathing a word of what they learned to anyone else in their department. The specialized knowledge they have acquired at such conferences and workshops is quietly added to their fund of personal expertise, enhancing their value and making them irreplaceable in their jobs.

This may also explain why many government officials who have been trained in the use of a specialized system, such as a database or accounting system, are often reluctant to provide basic training so that others in the office might become competent in the use of the system. As a result, there is often no backup for them when they are absent from work. When a colleague and I were visiting offices to obtain data for a study on performance management that we had been asked to do, we would all too often leave an office empty-handed because the individual who managed the data was not available and no one else had any idea how to provide what we needed. In the absence of the "expert" we could find no one who could access the data systems that had been set up to ensure reliable information on education or health services.

Westerners often think of this as a management problem, but its roots lie much deeper. The problem stems from a fundamental cultural difference in the way that information is viewed and the extent to which it should be shared. For Micronesians, information retains much of its traditional value as a prestige item, a private possession to be dispensed cautiously and in a measured way. For westerners, information (unlike wealth) is a commodity that they can afford to share generously. Indeed, they think of themselves as having the obligation to do so.

In the Micronesian world, information can be converted into social capital, just as wealth can. But the norms that govern the liberal use of information and wealth could not be more different.

《 • 《 • 《   6   》 • 》 • 》

Deciphering the Unspoken

What Silence Might Mean

*As the fifth-grade teacher asked her class the question she had
told them to prepare for, her eyes fell on the boy in the back row.
His name was Mariano, she knew, and he had come from one
of those islands in Micronesia. She was getting more and more
of those island students in her class each year—shy kids who
dressed a little differently from everyone else and kept pretty
much to themselves. Now and then they could be gently coaxed
out of their shells, but they would retreat into their own world
again soon afterward. She wanted to help them, but their parents
never seemed to attend PTA meetings or come to consult with the
teachers on the progress of their children. If only they came to
seek assistance, she was sure that she and the other teachers could
work with them to ensure that their children made up some of the
ground they had to cover to catch up with everyone else in the
class.*

*Her eyes scanned the class before they rested on Mariano in
the back row. He seemed quite bright even though he never volunteered an answer in the class. Sometimes hands would go up all
over the room, but never Mariano's. Well, here was a chance to
get the boy back in the game, to build up his confidence in himself and let others see what he could do. "Mariano," she asked,
"what is the planet closest to the sun?"*

*At the mention of his name, the boy dropped his eyes. The
teacher waited for a while, but there was no response. When she
repeated the question, Mariano simply shook his head from side*

*to side. Did that mean that he didn't know, the teacher wondered,
or whether he just didn't want to answer the question? These
island children are so strange, she thought.*

Communication across cultures involves weighing the meaning of
words in their context, but it also means interpreting silences and the
pauses in speech. Sometimes the gaps in speech, joined with facial
expressions and bodily gestures, speak more eloquently than words—
at least for one who can interpret what is being communicated.

Mariano's silence may be partly due to personal shyness and the
strangeness of his new situation at the school, but there are cultural
factors that could also help explain his reticence. Most young Micronesians have already learned that it is risky to call attention to oneself,
even by volunteering to answer a question in class. If Mariano had
given the wrong answer, he would have exposed himself to ridicule
from his teacher and his classmates. Yet, if he had the correct answer,
he might have been criticized for attempting to stand out. Either way
he would have been taking a risk. The safer course, as all young islanders learn, is to maintain a stony silence.

For a person to make a blatant attempt to get ahead individually
is to invite opprobrium in Micronesia. From the time they are toddlers, children are told that it is the tallest tree that is in danger of
being struck by lightning. The crab that struggles farthest up the side
of the pot to free itself from the hot water will be pulled down by all
the rest. For an individual to stand out from the rest is a challenge to
the "society first" order of values that is expected to be shared by all
in the community.

Bragging or overt self-aggrandizement is always in bad taste in the
islands. Any individual is expected to let his deeds speak for themselves. Even when he is praised for what he has done, he is expected
to dismiss the achievements as too ordinary to warrant such praise. A
verbal pat on the head by a well-intentioned teacher can cause problems for a student. Peace Corps volunteers teaching in Chuuk some
years ago used to complain that they didn't know how to react appropriately when a student distinguished himself or herself in class. Many
of them had already gone through the painful experience of praising
a student publicly in class only to find that their star student soon
afterward began to plummet in class performance. They used to joke

among themselves that their adulation was the best way to ruin the education of a fine student. What might have served as positive reinforcement for the student in educational situations back in the United States somehow turned into just the opposite in the islands.

During my teaching years at Xavier High School, I learned to save my words of praise for private sessions with the student after school when he and I could get a better sense of how he was reacting to the course and other features of school life. At least, the words of encouragement I had to offer him in private would not make him appear, in front of his classmates, as though he were the tallest tree in the forest or the crab who had almost reached the top of the pot.

Moreover, as a typical young Micronesian, Mariano would not have been prepared to share his personal problems with his teacher. His parents would probably have had the same reluctance to discuss their concerns over Mariano's school performance with his teachers. Such conversations demand the sort of trust that might require months or even years to build up. In addition, islanders are extremely hesitant to talk openly about family problems with anyone outside the family. To do so is seen almost as a betrayal of their own family. This, of course, only magnifies the natural reluctance they would already feel to express any negative feelings for fear that word of what they said might get back to their family and serve to intensify their problems. Consequently, school administrators and counselors who attempt to probe into family problems with the best of intentions are usually frustrated when they try to talk to students experiencing difficulty in school. More often than not, they find themselves as much in the dark after their attempts to talk through these problems with students as they were before the conversation began.

Even in our boarding school at Xavier, where students and faculty lived together and developed close ties, teasing out such information was extremely difficult. One young man, I remember, had been acting with uncharacteristic belligerence toward his fellow students for over a month as his grades dropped sharply. It was clear that something was bothering him, but no one on the faculty knew what the problem was. We might never have known if a student close to this young man had not approached one of the staff and told him. The young man had just discovered that the man he had always believed to be his father was not his real father after all. It was only then that the staff could begin to address the personal crisis, but even so we had to enlist the help of his friends to get him through the trouble. In other situations like this, as when a student had a serious falling out with his cousin, also a student at the school, we staff members had to rely on the assistance of other students to fill us in on the background and to act as "guardian angels," or peer counselors, for the students afterward.

The reticence of islanders about family problems extends well beyond students like these. A health aide working in the local hospital once told us what happened when he examined young girls for pregnancy. Some of the girls were very young, even as young as thirteen or fourteen years old, he said. After testing them for pregnancy, he would have to inform the girls of the results of their tests. When a girl was told that she was pregnant, she would almost always drop her head with her eyes fixed steadily on the ground. As his follow-up question, the health aide would ask the girl if the father of the child was someone in her family. She would never answer directly, of course, but the sure sign of an affirmative was when the girl would drop her head even lower and maintain a fierce silence. Her silence to that question was as certain an answer as if she had nodded up and down and shouted *yes*. Family problems may not be a subject for open conversation, but there are other ways of finding out what one needs to know.

It should go without saying, then, that hotlines—for drinking problems, spouse abuse, or anything else—are never going to be successful in the islands. To expect an islander, who knows a good percentage of the people on the island, to offer the intimate details of his own life and possibly his dealings with his family to a person manning the hotline is hard to imagine. The strategy depends on two most improbable assumptions: that the person calling on the hotline in a tiny island society can ever expect to be anonymous, and that the caller, even if he were somehow to remain anonymous, would be willing to share such personal information with someone outside his intimate family circle. The same holds true for Alcoholics Anonymous or other twelve-step programs that require people to share personal details of their life with a group of others. These programs might have great success in the United States and other large modern countries, but they have never proved effective in Micronesia and probably never will.

Fig. 8. Pohnpeian elder: "Like the silence of a barracuda" (1975).
Courtesy of Carlos Viti.

Speaking to People Rather Than about Things

The new Peace Corps volunteer was clearly exasperated as he slumped into a chair at the lounge while other volunteers leafed through magazines and engaged in idle chatter. "What's wrong, Rick?" one of them asked. "You seem stressed."

The new volunteer then launched into his harangue. He began with an account of a local man who had shown great enthusiasm over his plans to set up a wind generator on his island. The man had become a good friend of his during his first two months in the village, chatting over coffee in the evening for hours. The man had helped him with his language study, explained some of the customs that baffled the volunteer, and introduced him to many other people on the island. The two of them had become close friends—or so the young volunteer thought. The volunteer had come to rely on his Micronesian friend for support and encouragement.

Then the time had come for him to begin serious work on the wind generator project. One evening he confided in his friend his plans to proceed with the first steps in getting the wind generator built. But before he did that, he would have to get permission from an older man in the village to have the generator set up on his land. As the volunteer outlined his plans, his local friend made a great show of support, cheering the volunteer on as he described what he was going to do. Finally, the volunteer suggested that they see the landowner the next day. Would his friend meet him the following morning so that together they could go over to the landowner's house and get the permission he needed to set up the generator on his land? The friend agreed to meet him the next morning at nine so that they could do this.

The next day the volunteer waited for his friend to appear. Nine o'clock passed, but his friend did not appear. The volunteer waited for two more hours, but still his friend failed to show up. Perhaps something unexpected had come up, the volunteer thought, so when he met his friend that evening he suggested that they reschedule for the next day. His friend enthusiastically agreed, but he never showed up that day either, or the next day.

The volunteer was dejected when he met his fellow volunteers

*in the lounge. He felt betrayed, as he explained to the room full
of Americans. "What is it with this place? How could my friend
promise me that he would come with me when he had no intention of showing up? Don't these people here ever mean what they
say?"*

Words in cross-cultural situations don't always carry the meanings we might assume they do, as the American volunteer learned in
his dealings with his Micronesian friend. Did his friend mean what
he said? Yes, but he was responding to the American on an entirely
different plane. His yes was meant to affirm his support of his young
American friend, even though he was fully aware of the difficulty
that he would have in keeping the appointment. Possibly the man
anticipated resistance from the landowner that the volunteer would
not have known about. Or perhaps he was a junior relative of the
landowner's and recognized that it would be socially improper to ask
him for the use of his family's land. Could the Micronesian have even
begun to explain the intricacies of a situation like this to an American
who knew almost nothing about the culture? Was his yes a deliberate
attempt to mislead his young American friend? Or was it simply a way
of assuring him of his friendship and support, whatever difficulties he
might have in pursuing the course of action the volunteer had already
laid out for him?

It's all about people, as might be expected in a Pacific island culture. Anyone who has lived in the islands for any length of time can
rattle off numerous experiences similar to that of the volunteer in this
vignette. We can all recount the times we've felt duped by someone
who has made what we understood to be a commitment but failed to
carry it out. There are appointments made but not kept, pledges to
do something that was left undone, promises of assistance that was
never given. It's easy to attribute this to the easygoing ways of islanders, or perhaps the unsatisfactory work ethic that prevails. But more
often than not, the real issue lies elsewhere. Island people have a way
of speaking to the person rather than about the particular matter at
hand. They don't want to disappoint a person who is making a request
of them. If yes is what someone wants to hear, yes is what he will hear.
After all, islanders desperately want to make people feel good.

Sometimes the noes island people offer to requests are just as confusing. Once, while living in a Chuukese village during my early years of language study, I offered some food to a young man who had helped me all day long. He was not hungry, he replied. Half an hour later I found the man lying on the ground outside the house unconscious after he had fainted from what others told me was hunger. He had not eaten all day, it turned out, but still felt obliged to make the polite refusal of the food that he so badly wanted. His no didn't really mean no, just as yes doesn't always mean yes. If I had been more observant and better schooled in Micronesian ways, I would have understood that I was expected to press the food on him and insist that he eat. If I had, my hungry friend would have gratefully eaten. His no was simply good manners in an island society in which it is thought rude to appear greedy.

So yes doesn't always mean yes, nor does no always mean no. If "truth" is conditional on the maintenance of smooth relationships with the parties involved, how do we find the answer to the questions we might ask? Naturally, an awareness of the cultural context in which our conversation partner finds himself is the best way of anticipating a problem, although many westerners will be unequipped to take stock of this context. Even so, there are other ways of reading responses as well. Verbal cues are not the only or even the most important ones in gauging responses. Timing can reveal a great deal, too. When the pause before the inevitable yes is a beat longer than usual, this could be a signal that the person might have trouble holding up his end of the bargain. One strategy is to begin listening less and watching more—scanning the face for the degree of enthusiasm registered, checking for subtle signs of concern.

The strong aversion of islanders to offending anyone frequently takes another form. When they walk into an unfamiliar situation and meet people they don't know, Micronesians are hesitant to talk freely. Instead, they adopt a slow and noncommittal approach that allows them time to scout out the social terrain so that they can avoid pitfalls. They will try to find out who is related to whom, who holds what position on anything, and what subjects are safe to discuss so that they can proceed without giving offense to anyone. They will generally explore the terrain well before making a strong commitment on any subject. This slow conversational dance permits them to plot the newcomers on their social map and so avoid embarrassing their guests.

Less of great substance may be discussed, but at least they will have shown basic courtesy to those in their midst. Conversation is, after all, less about things than for people.

My experience has taught me to look for one of the women if ever I wish to get a direct reading of where I stand with a family. A few years ago, as I attended the inauguration of a governor on one island, I found myself talking amiably with a traditional chief even though he knew that I was openly critical of his position on one important issue. His wife, however, refused to greet me when I approached her in the reception line. A church leader who is a friend of mine had a similar experience. He was pointedly and rudely ignored by a woman who thought that he had taken action against someone in her family, even though her husband chatted with the church leader in an easy and friendly fashion. Again and again I have heard of situations like these. It seems that women are a better gauge to where one stands with a family than men. Men often maintain a polite and deferential stance, even toward those they do not like, while women are more likely to show their genuine feelings.

All this presents a problem for westerners who are charged with the responsibility of finding out what island people are thinking. What are their hopes and fears? What are their aspirations? What are the difficulties they face? How are we going to be able to help, they ask themselves, unless the islanders are more forthcoming? We're coming into the situation blind and won't be able to provide assistance if the persons with whom we speak don't provide the information we need. Let it all hang out, Americans helpfully suggest. But can Micronesians, who come from a very different tradition, one in which they speak more to affirm people than to package information, really be expected to do so?

Social Signals

Every so often the American teacher was invited to parties, where he would marvel at the way islanders seemed to anticipate every need. A napkin? A second serving of meat or fish? A second glass of iced tea or beer? A bowl of water for washing his hands at the end of the meal? He had it before he could even ask for it, sometimes even before he himself realized that he wanted it. It was almost as if the hosts considered it a matter of pride to provide their guest everything needed before the guest could articulate his desire. Like other newcomers to the island, the teacher attributed all this to the superb hospitality of the island people. After all, they were acclaimed for their graciousness to visitors. But people's uncanny ability to anticipate the needs of others extended well beyond all this. If you entered a room at which three people sat around a table, a fourth chair would be placed in front of you instantaneously. If you appeared at the doorway of a room in which a group of young people was listening to the radio, a hand would reach out to turn down the volume even before you could make your request.

The teacher only realized how much he had come to appreciate this quality in its absence. In his occasional visits to the United States, he found himself taken by surprise at the degree to which his fellow Americans seem to expect him to verbalize everything. "How are you feeling today?" "Do you want something to eat?" "What do you think of our new house?" Must Americans demand verbal answers for everything? Didn't his own people ever do what islanders were so skilled at doing—scan the scene for visual clues to find the answers themselves? Could it be that the very people who thought of themselves as owning a permanent perch at the pinnacle of development were retarded or blind? Why hadn't they mastered the skills in which unschooled islanders excelled?

Years later, the teacher stood at the doorway of the TV room in his own house, crowded with young Americans, teachers as young as he had been when he first came to the island. They sprawled on the lounge chairs in the room, with one of them using the only unoccupied seat to prop up his legs. The teacher stood there silently, waiting for someone to move. One . . . two . . . three . . . four . . . five minutes elapsed before one of the young Americans turned to him to ask if he wanted a chair. If the old teacher had any doubts that his experience in Micronesia had changed his expectations and the way he viewed life, they were removed then and there. He declined the chair, slowly turned to leave, and realized how much of a stranger he had become to his own culture.

The passage above is taken from an article that I wrote a couple of years ago to illustrate the lessons that expatriates who have spent time in the islands can learn from Micronesians. Islanders are masters in scanning the social environment, picking up clues, and responding to them. From early childhood Micronesians are trained to be attuned to social signals. They develop an instinct for sensing approval or disapproval even when this may not be overtly expressed. In the same way they develop an acute sense of the needs of others even when these are not articulated.

Anyone who has had the experience of being hosted by Micronesians can resonate with the passage quoted above. Almost never would a guest have to ask for anything because it was always provided in advance. I once remember thinking, at the end of another one of those feasts that island people passed off as an ordinary dinner, how nice it would be to have a little water with which to clean my hands. No sooner had I started to enunciate my request "*Kese mochen kepwe...*" ("Could you please...") than the basin and towel appeared. It almost seemed to be an exercise in mind reading, or perhaps a contest between guest and hosts over who was quicker on the draw. If it was a contest, then the hosts almost always won.

This sixth sense appears even when islanders are not in the role of hosts. Often when I've been in a situation in which I need to talk to one person alone, the others in the room will begin excusing themselves to allow for a private conversation, even if no one has explicitly asked them to leave. Whenever I've gone to another island with island friends, they will always make sure that the shower house in the place we're staying is equipped with soap, has a full bucket of water ready, and has doors that can be tightly closed. The ability of islanders to take stock of a situation and to provide instantaneously for the needs of others is amazing, especially when compared with the response of a westerner in the same situation. "Do you need soap?" they might ask, or "Do you want the shower door locked?" These are regarded as superfluous questions in Micronesia.

But person-oriented societies have their drawbacks even on such matters as this. Many of the young islanders who attended our boarding school in Chuuk or the minor seminary we ran on Guam seemed to have problems concentrating on their studies. Even if they were repeatedly told to focus their energies entirely on the book or paper in front of them, they seemed to have difficulty in narrowing their focus on the task at hand. An experienced teacher once suggested that perhaps the diffused awareness that allows island students to pick up social signals so easily also makes it difficult for them to block out what Americans might consider extraneous "noise" and focus intently on a single subject.

Just as Micronesians pick up social signals without the need for verbal expression, they also communicate emotional signals of their own without resorting to words. Often enough these are transmitted by facial gestures or even pauses. Both of these can be just as easily misunderstood by someone outside the culture as an islander's yes or no.

Take the smile, for instance. Many of us raised in a culture in which people smile when they are pleased and frown when they are confused or dismayed fail to realize that the trademark Micronesian smile can be an ambiguous sign. It might be an indication of happiness, an expression that all is well, but it could serve other purposes, too. The smile can be used to cover embarrassment, as expatriate teachers soon come to realize, when students are called on in class and are forced to admit in front of their classmates that they don't know the answer. Basketball players who miss an easy lay-up shot will smile, as will baseball players who let an easy ground ball slip between their legs. A young man who drops a heavy load he's carrying before he can get it on the back of the pickup truck might flash a big smile at those watching.

An American once told me about the time he had fallen clumsily on his backside, twisting his leg behind him as he went down. As he heard the echoes of laughter from those watching him take the spill, he could feel his own rising indignation and then outright anger at the Micronesian spectators for making a fool of him. Polite people weren't supposed to laugh at the misfortunes of others, he had always been taught. It was only much later that he came to understand that smiles and laughter serve another purpose: they put people at ease and deflect embarrassment when something awkward happens. It was only then that he understood that the islanders had not been laughing at him, but laughing with him—at least if he had accepted their invitation to join in the fun.

Pauses can represent another cultural stumbling block for expatriates. When I was in charge of Xavier High School, I noticed that the young Micronesians on the staff began regularly sitting at their own table for meals. Because my hope had always been for a socially integrated faculty, I made it a point to talk with some of the Micronesian faculty and chide them for their clannishness. One of them replied that they wanted to talk more, but they found this hard to do when sitting with Americans. It wasn't just that the U.S. volunteers were conversing about football games and Thanksgiving celebrations and other subjects of little interest to islanders. Even when discussing matters of mutual interest—classroom problems and campus gossip—the Micronesians felt frozen out of the conversation. Upon further investigation, it was easy to see why. When the young Americans finished their thoughts, they would pause a beat or two to signify that the floor was now open for anyone else who wanted to contribute. If no one took up the offer, they would begin to chatter away in an effort to avoid what would have been for them a painful silence. Micronesian teachers, on the other hand, were politely waiting for them to finish what they had to say—but they waited for four or five beats to make sure the speaker was finished before they would respond. The length of the pauses in conversation was the cultural issue that frustrated both groups. Americans thought they had given time for island teachers to make a contribution, while Micronesians waited in vain for what they considered a decent interval before launching their own comments.

All that is *said* is not necessarily *spoken,* as we can see. If cultural misunderstanding can arise over spoken language, it can just as easily occur over silences and gestures. Indeed, it can be sparked by the inability to read social situations correctly. To learn the local language requires not just mastering a vocabulary and the rules for how to use it, but understanding the meanings of body language and facial gestures. Deciphering the unspoken is an essential skill for Micronesians and those hoping to communicate effectively with them.

« · « · « 7 » · » · »

Showing Respect

It All Begins in the Family

The father and mother and children are sitting on the floor for the evening meal. With them are three other adults, close relatives also living in the household: the mother's unmarried sister and a younger married couple in their mid-twenties related to the father. Pots of food are set on the floor in the middle of the loose circle. Two toddlers are being fed by the mother from her own plate. Meanwhile, the other children sit waiting until the adults have served themselves before they start to put food on their own plates. The children are mostly silent, now and then one of them whispering something to another. A teenage boy is sitting on one side of the room as far from his fifteen-year-old sister as he can get in the crowded room.

When the meal is finished, the mother beckons her older daughter and two other girls, seven and nine, to help clean up. The teenage boy, who has never looked entirely comfortable, jumps up and leaves to join his friends outside, while his two younger brothers glance at him enviously. As the mother supervises the cleanup, her sister takes charge of one of the toddlers and places the other in the arms of an eleven-year-old girl. The father, in need of a smoke, sends out one of the younger sons for a pack of cigarettes from the nearby village store. Another family meal is finished.

Respect is one of the central concepts in island culture; the word is forever being used in the islands. The importance of respect is a lesson that Micronesians begin to absorb within the circle of their family from the youngest age. Children learn to show respect for their parents and other elders in the family, waiting until older people have helped themselves to food and carrying out assigned tasks in the household as instructed. The mother's adult sister is entitled to nearly as much respect from the children as their mother. The children in a village family would have called her "Mama" just as they would their own mother. Likewise, children would have referred to older male relatives as "Papa" while treating them as such.

Almost as soon as the young could walk and begin to take care of themselves, they might be put in charge of a younger brother or sister. It was common to see a young girl carrying a child not much younger than herself. The girl might be expected to keep a close watch on the child for much of the day, bathing and feeding the child and handing it back to the mother when asked. At times, the girl might pass off her burden to a sister slightly younger than herself, just as a boy might ask his younger brother to do a task that he had been given. When a child was given a responsibility such as this, he was in no position to refuse the older person to whom he owed respect, but he could pass the burden down the family hierarchical chain to the child at the bottom of the line. After all, age was very important in Micronesian culture. It had just as much bearing on who was entitled to respect in the family as it did in the culture at large.

Visitors to Micronesia who enter a village home expecting a loose and easygoing air are usually surprised at what they find. The tight organization in the family with its clear lines of authority is evident in even the simplest household. Although there may seem to be children everywhere, the family still impresses most of us as much more disciplined than the western family. Children talk to one another quietly, lapsing into silence when the adults are carrying on a discussion among themselves. It is rare to find children quarreling with one another or a child shouting his insistent demands to his parents—the type of unruliness that is a major part of the life of any American family. This often comes as a great surprise to outsiders, who expect to encounter the chaos of an American household in a family as large as many island families are. Instead, the family scene is a throwback to what might have been found years ago during their grandfather's or great-grandfather's time, when parental discipline was strong and unapologetic and when honor was still paid to the saying: "Children should be seen and not heard."

If deference to age was inbred into Micronesians, so too was a strong distinction between gender lines in the family. Some years ago when I was conducting interviews with families, I would often ask about the birth rank of a child. My question was met more often than not with a puzzled look. "Do you mean birth rank among *all* the children?" some would ask. Then they would silently calculate the answer to a question that I assumed they could rattle off immediately. They could have told me instantly what the number of their child was among their daughters or among their sons, because the traditional Micronesian family would have kept the two gender lines distinct. Why? Because the roles, and to a great extent their expectations, of children of the two genders were very different. So was the respect that each paid to the other. The difference became all the more pronounced as children aged.

As boys in a family reach the age of adolescence, their relationship with one another becomes more formal and distant. The casual friendship between two teenage brothers that we might expect in a western family is conspicuously absent in the Micronesian family. Brothers avoid one another as they get older because, in the formal age-ranked system of the island family, deference is expected to be given or received. I often noticed in Chuuk that when young men went out for a night of drinking and adventure, they would choose as their companions cousins and other distant relatives in preference to their own brothers. Then I began to realize that the same was true in other islands. This was only to be expected. How could a young person relax in the presence of his brother when one was always conscious of owing respect to the other due to the importance that age continued to have in island families?

Girls in the family may have the same problem, but they usually are not as successful in avoiding one another since they have to do the work around the house and so are constantly in one another's presence. At such close quarters, they constantly face the risk of confrontation, a battle between unequals. Younger girls must be prepared to be scolded or even slapped by their older sisters. When circumstances allow, it is easier for them simply to avoid one another or to go about their work silently.

The relationship between brothers and sisters, especially after adolescence, is even more problematic. Although they were expected to care for one another, their dealings within and outside the family were constrained by formalities that prevented them from engaging in anything that would suggest an intimate relationship between them. (We will examine this in more detail in the next chapter.) They did not engage in easy banter, they certainly did not express any close affection, and their time together was limited. Overall, they were encouraged to avoid one another as much as possible, even within the family circle.

The relationship between siblings, like the relationship between parents and children, was marked by respect. This often surprises outsiders who expect to see in the family the kind of casual association that is to be found in the West. Particularly after adolescence, there is not the easy familiarity that we might expect of such warm and outgoing island people. Indeed, I have often been surprised to find out years later that two individuals I had come to know separately were siblings, so well concealed was their relationship to each other.

Silence and distance have always been the main markers of respect in any Micronesian culture. Both are practiced throughout the islands even today both within the family and in the broader community. Silence can mean holding one's tongue in the presence of another to whom respect is due, but it might also mean not interrupting a person and certainly not contradicting anyone with authority. Hence, conversation at Micronesian family gatherings will not flow as easily as it might in the West.

Respect is also shown by maintaining a distance, vertically as well as horizontally, from a person. In traditional times this meant that people were sometimes obliged to lower their body or even crawl in the presence of a chief or elder. Today it means simply keeping one's body bent and the head low. The distance symbolizing respect was also horizontal, so that people attempting to show respect for someone would stand off a bit to avoid crowding. In some cases, respect dictated that the person remove himself altogether from the presence of a person. Avoidance of this kind was an important element in traditional respect. Respect was due not just to chiefs and public figures, but even to older siblings, as we have seen. Younger brothers were to keep a respectful distance from their older brothers, and boys were to

Fig. 9. Government official greeting the chief on Woleai (ca. 1970).
Courtesy of Greg Trifonovich.

maintain a distance from their sisters after puberty. Often this trans-
lated into minimizing any personal contact whatsoever with the individual.

This is changing, of course, in modernized families in town where
there is much more chumminess between family members, even
between parents and their children. Age ranking remains important
even in these families, but the young interact with one another with
a greater degree of freedom. Respectful silence and avoidance are less
strictly observed than in the traditional island family. There we may
see the more open type of family interaction, with the teasing and
quarrels between children, that reminds us of home.

Dissent with Deference

*The traditional meetinghouse was filled with people who had
come to celebrate a feast given in honor of the Nahnmwarki, or
paramount chief of that section of Pohnpei. High titles had been*

bestowed on two men in the community, and this feast was the
public acknowledgment of the honor the two had received. The
Nahnmwarki was seated at the center of the U-shaped platform
in front of the crowd, with two men crouching at his side to serve
him. On either side of the front of the platform sat the two men
who had just received titles. Below, in the body of the meeting-
house, men pounded sakau at four large stones as other people
milled around. Outside were piled the carcasses of freshly slaugh-
tered pigs and the yams and sakau that would be presented to the
dignitaries.

The murmur of the people quieted as one of the new titlehold-
ers came forward and began to speak. He began with the usual
formal respectful greetings to the Nahnmwarki and to the others
who held the highest titles in the community before he launched
into the main part of his talk. He spoke for a few minutes about a
program that he hoped to launch in an effort to help people mar-
ket their produce in town so that the families might earn some
money. As he spoke, Marcus, one of the men assigned to attend
the chief, lowered his eyes and his jaw stiffened a bit. Marcus was
no friend of the speaker. He knew that the project of which the
titleholder spoke was intended to benefit his own family and that
very little of the funds he had received to get the project under
way went to anyone else in the community. Yet, Marcus nodded
with everyone else as the speaker went on to enumerate the ben-
efits that everyone would receive from the project. At one point
he tilted his head upward and caught the eye of his wife, sitting
to one side in the gathering. He raised his eyebrows slightly and
noticed the tight smile of his wife. Then he lowered his head and
listened impassively to the rest of the talk.

The patterns of respect behavior learned within the family are
practiced in broader society. This vignette illustrates the importance
of showing overt deference to chiefs and those who hold high titles on
Pohnpei. But it also suggests some of the subtle ways in which people
might make their genuine feelings known, if only to their spouse. In
other island groups, respect must publicly be shown traditional leaders, although there may be differences in the way deference is shown.

A highly respected village chief in Chuuk once stood up to give a speech in a meetinghouse. As he began to speak, he started laying out a course of action for the village that he had not yet vetted with his people. Men shook their heads up and down as if in agreement with the chief as he went on to describe his plan, but small pockets of people began loudly whispering among themselves their own reactions. As the chief continued with his speech, he began altering the action plan he proposed. In the end, the chief was offering his people a substantially different plan from the one he had originally been proposing. No one had been so rude as to shout him down or voice publicly their opposition to the plan, but they had made clear by their murmured reaction their thinking. The chief had the good sense to incorporate into his plan the desires of his people, as any traditional authority holder in Micronesia would have been expected to do.

The same respect patterns, along with the subtle ways of showing a difference of opinion, are carried over into government and business today. Authority figures in either the traditional or modern sphere are accorded the outward respect due them. Failure to do so would result in loss of face for the chief or public official, and no islander would want to be charged with that offense. The art of conducting oneself properly in an island setting consists in allowing the one in authority to retain his *bella figura,* while still registering one's dissent in an acceptably subtle fashion. To act otherwise could be a declaration of war against the public figure that would more often than not prove counterproductive.

Once at a meeting of educators, I listened to an elected official explain his strategy for improvement of the troubled public education system. He told us in the course of his talk that he was fully committed to implementing the government decision to upgrade the credentials of all public school teachers. Within the next two years all elementary school teachers would be required to obtain a two-year college degree. When he finished, there was a smattering of appreciative response from the others sitting around the room. Any hesitation the listeners expressed was about how this reform could be carried out in such a short period of time. When it was time for me to respond, I boldly suggested that even if his reform strategy were fully implemented it still would not bring about the desired results. The failure of the education system, I suggested, was due to other problems, ones he had not addressed. There was an almost audible gasp from some of those in the room. The public official, who was used to dealing with recalcitrant Americans, announced that the law was the law and that he would ensure that it was obeyed. That was that. I had wantonly disregarded the unwritten rule of public discussion, and he put me in my place.

Island events are conducted with a certain formality. They are not the type of town hall meetings once common in the United States at which everyone is free to express directly his unvarnished opinion. There is seldom an outward show of disagreement; any difference of opinion will be masked.

If a person wishes to reply to someone in authority who has made a statement, he will usually begin with a statement expressing a positive reaction toward what the person has said, only then continuing to suggest politely that he would like to broaden the view presented. He might go on to introduce considerations that the speaker had not addressed, carefully suggesting a way in which the conclusions that the former speaker made could be modified. In other words, he builds on what has been said rather than take issue with it.

There are other ways in which dissent can be expressed without being articulated. Sometimes people show their lack of enthusiasm for a proposal by sitting with head down and keeping the face expressionless. At other times it may be through a voiced approval that is without any hint of enthusiasm. Often their objection is conveyed indirectly through the questions they ask. Whatever the method used, any expressions of dissent will be suggested rather than flatly stated. The purpose of the exercise is to show proper deference to the authority so that he will never publicly lose face. For that reason, the type of free exchange of opinion so common in the West is not often found in island societies—whether in the boardroom, the conference room, or the traditional meetinghouse.

In view of the importance of respect for authority in Micronesia, anything that may be considered a breach of loyalty is repugnant to islanders. The ethical codes that are supposed to govern the conduct of public servants, for instance, may be honored by most employees, but only rarely will these principles trump the sense of personal loyalty they feel toward their boss. To expect civil servants to honor these principles above the persons for whom they work is simply unrealistic, given the way an island society operates. However many appeals are made to employees or others to dial a public number to inform the government of specific abuse occurring in the government, response is nearly null. Any employee would have to shed the ingrained schooling in respect he has acquired from childhood; he would have to fore-swear the importance of personal respect due his supervisor, before he could become a whistle-blower.

Trade-Offs in Respect Today

The meetinghouse was packed with people attending the feast. The high chief sat in his usual place in the center of the elevated platform, while the master of ceremonies ushered in the men bearing litters with slaughtered pigs and other food offerings. People inside the meetinghouse stirred with expectation, for the wealthiest man in that part of the island had been given a high title. This feast was the recipient's traditional gesture of respect to the chief, the customary thank-you for the honor. Somehow the people gathered in the meetinghouse that day believed that the event would be a little more than the usual symbolic gesture prescribed by the culture. The businessman had almost promised them as much when he had hinted to his friends about his plans for the day.

The people outside the meetinghouse were startled by a loud rumble. They turned to see a brand new Toyota edging into the clearing in front of the building near the pile of slit pigs and cut poles used to carry the pigs into the meetinghouse. As the truck came to a stop, people darted out to see what was going on. They smiled at one another in appreciation of the truck and its contents. On the bed in the back of the truck was a high pile of cartons—food of every kind that must have cleared many of the shelves of the businessman's large store.

A few minutes later the businessman walked to the front of the meetinghouse, bowed respectfully to the high chief, and with his head still bowed presented the keys for the Toyota pickup to the high chief.

The manner in which respect is shown to authorities is being altered in today's society, as this vignette suggests. Chiefs and traditional leaders once received gifts of food, most of which was promptly redistributed to members of the community. The food offered to an authority figure in the past was certainly a token of respect, given in recognition of his status in the community—but it was also something more. It was a form of tax that could be used to advance projects initiated by the chief for the benefit of the entire community. The gift of food or other items could be used by the chief to reward those making significant contributions to the village.

In the vignette above, the chief is handed the keys to a pickup truck filled with store-bought goods. This represents a new form of paying tribute, or manifesting respect, to a chief that is very different from the old forms. In the end, the truck and perhaps much of the tinned goods will remain in his hands rather than be redistributed for the benefit of the community. Today it is increasingly common for traditional chiefs on Pohnpei to be honored with cash or purchased gifts rather than with the produce of the land. In return for a traditional title, a successful businessman or political leader might offer the paramount chief a check for a few thousand dollars. This transaction, which often seems to be nothing less than the crass purchase of a title, can be seen in a slightly different light. It can be viewed as an exchange between an authority in the customary sphere and one in the business sphere. The businessman who receives the title is offered a solid footing in traditional society, while the chief who bestows the title is offered the means to help position himself in the modern cash economy. For each party the range for respect is widened.

The way in which respect is being shown to other figures of authority is also changing today. When church leaders go to celebrate services at another church upon the regular rotation of pastors, they may return with a truck piled high with household goods and food. Such gifts, too, are a sign of respect paid to church authorities. Elected political figures, on the other hand, can not accept such monetary tokens of respect without the risk of indictment for accepting bribes.

Such concerns would not have arisen in a traditional island society where the forms of respect, as well as the obligations of the authorities to the people they served, were well established. In today's society, however, the boundaries between different spheres is still being negotiated. To what extent should respect for traditional leaders be carried over into the modern political system? What about church leaders and those individuals who have distinguished themselves in business? Should the respect for them be extended to the political arena when they attempt to rally support for a political candidate or run for office themselves? These are questions that confound fully modernized western societies. It is no surprise that they continue to bewilder island societies that have only recently adopted a modern form of government.

Decades ago, when the U.S. first introduced the new system of representative government into Micronesia, people elected many of their traditional leaders into the legislature, but they soon found this system unworkable. After a process of trial and error, people seemed to come to the conclusion that the legislatures could not function as they were intended if the chiefs did all the talking and the commoners remained respectfully silent. Oil and water don't mix, they evidently decided. Consequently, no special accommodations were offered traditional leaders in the modern government system except in the Marshalls, where the *irooj*, or paramount chiefs, have retained a largely honorific role in a separate house of the national legislature. Elsewhere, traditional leaders may run for elected office if they wish, but there is no guarantee that their customary title will be enough to win the seat.

This brings us to the final and possibly the most controversial way in which respect may be converted into the currency of today's world—something that the West dismisses as nepotism. Favoritism toward family in awarding jobs or services to family members is frequently targeted by westerners, and occasionally by islanders themselves, as one of the most flagrant violations of the standards of good governance. When a person in charge of a government department offers a job in his office to a relative, this is usually dismissed as another instance of relatives taking care of one another in the usual island style. This could be seen as sharing the wealth with those to whom one is indebted, especially members of one's own family. For a person in authority to choose relatives to fill salaried positions can be understood merely as a way of meeting social obligations to those close to him. In a society woven so tightly with personal relationships, it is not easy to make evenhanded choices that accord with the western principles of good government. "Taking care of your own" is the judgment usually offered in cases where a person hires someone in his family.

But there is another part of the picture that westerners don't always see. I didn't see it either until an encounter with an uneducated Chuukese employee of the Catholic mission stopped me in my tracks twenty years ago. When I asked this man to find two strong young men to trim some trees on the property, he brought in his son and nephew to do the job. They completed the work quickly and well, but I couldn't help teasing the man a few days later when he came in to pick up their pay. "So, you ended up hiring your own relatives, just as so many people in the government are accused of doing?" I taunted him. He explained that hiring his own younger relatives made good sense for him because it was easier to get them to do what he wanted. If they slacked off he could scold them. He could hold them accountable for quality work and insist that they finish the job on time. All of this was possible because as junior members of his own family they owed him respect anyway. He was warning me that what I would have called nepotism was in this case a sensible strategy for building on the respect the young men owed him in order to get the job done.

One of the very best public elementary schools on Pohnpei made demands on its teachers that were almost unthinkable. Teachers were required to appear in the classroom each day, even during village funerals, when teachers in other schools would routinely skip class for two or three days. The same teachers were also required to remain at school until the end of the work day at 4:30 p.m., an hour or two after the last class had ended, to correct papers and prepare the next day's classes. Teacher absenteeism, a major problem nearly everywhere else, was unknown at this school. The high test scores of the eighth grade students and the remarkable acceptance rate into high school reflected the order and discipline that had become the hallmark of this school. What I only learned later, however, is that nearly all the teachers were junior relatives of the school principal, a man who also happened to hold the title of section chief in that part of the island. The teachers who took orders from this man were already bound, by virtue of family and community ties, to respect him. It would be hard to imagine any other principal, a person without the same title to respect from his teachers, being able to exercise the authority this man wielded to the clear advantage of the school and its students.

This is not to say that what others might call nepotism always works such wonders. In many instances, the result may be quite the

opposite: an incompetent and unmotivated individual may be draw-
ing a salary while contributing nothing at all to the people he should
be serving. But the selection of a close relative to fill a post offers the
supervisor a way of meeting obligations toward his own family, while
also allowing him to utilize to advantage the personal authority he
enjoys over his appointee. Under the best circumstances, the practice
builds on personal respect within the family to strengthen the authority of the person in the workplace.

Respect in the workplace today is not automatically bestowed on
those selected to supervise offices. Young, college-educated individuals may be selected on the basis of the skills they possess, but this
doesn't guarantee that those who work under them will show them
real respect. Those working under them will show formal deference,
of course, as islanders almost always do. Genuine respect in an island
society, however, is determined by age, family, and social status. If
the supervisor of an office cannot change the factors that determine
his own rank on the social map, he can at least make an attempt to
stack the office staff with people who must acknowledge his personal
authority over them. This provides some measure of respect until the
time when he can expect to achieve respect on his own merits. Thus,
what we in the West call nepotism can be seen as a strategy that, while
spreading the wealth among relatives, attempts to employ leverage to
achieve effective office management. While the dangers may outweigh
the benefits, the practice at least makes sense in the logic of island
culture.

« • « • « *8* » • » • »

The Matter of Sex

Taboos in the Family

*The Australian volunteer knew enough to take off his shoes
before he entered the village house. He hadn't been on the island
very long, but he prided himself on knowing at least a little about
island etiquette. He had been pleased when one of the star players on the high school basketball team he coached invited him to
join his family for dinner. He had never been inside a local house
before and he was looking forward to the opportunity to experience island living, at least for a few hours. So he took a seat on
the floor and waited until the food was brought in and the rest of
the family took their places on the floor.*

*After the family settled down and the guest was introduced to
the other members of the household, conversation was stilted for
a while. But that was to be expected, he thought, since most of
the others in the family had only a limited grasp of English. After
a while, though, the initial discomfort eased and it was beginning
to look as though everyone was starting to enjoy the evening. He
even found that he drew appreciative smiles as he launched into
a vivid description of the on-court heroics of the young athlete in
the family. Encouraged at this, he pointed at a ten-year-old boy
sitting across from him and predicted that he, too, had a great
future ahead of him as a basketball player. Then his eyes fell on
the boy's sister, a strikingly attractive girl of about eighteen, who
had said almost nothing up to this point. Perhaps a compliment
would help, he thought. "Your sister there is a real stunner," he*

said. "I bet all the blokes on the island are chasing her. I would myself if I were a little younger."

Instead of the laughter he expected, he saw everyone in the family stiffen. The girl attempted a small smile but immediately dropped her eyes. His star athlete looked confused. There was an awkward silence before the mother of the family suddenly rose and started collecting dishes. Slowly conversation resumed, but the mood had clearly changed now.

Some days later, when the Australian recounted all this to a friend who had been living on the island for almost three years, the friend laughed. "You didn't really say that, did you?" he asked. The Australian looked puzzled at the question. He insisted that his remark to the girl was mild compared to the lurid comments he had often heard groups of his teenage students make about some of the girls in their class. At this, his friend only shook his head and began to laugh some more.

Before the era of the modern concrete house, there was little privacy to be found in a Micronesian home. Aside from a small storage space in the back somewhere, the house was one large undivided room with almost no furniture. This single large space usually served as the dining area, the living room, and the dormitory as members of the household unfolded their sleeping mats and picked a place on the floor to take their rest. There were no personal quarters for anyone in this type of living situation. Clothes and a few personal items might be tucked away in a corner somewhere, but everyone shared the common space as best they could. Only as concrete houses became popular from the 1960s on would residences be divided into separate rooms. Today, in fact, the old single room style houses are still the rule in the atolls and the more remote villages.

Even though the traditional Micronesian family lived at close quarters, there were social boundaries between family members that were not to be crossed, as we have seen in the last chapter. Respect, rooted in age and gender, created those boundaries. Well-defined norms for addressing others in the family were observed, and certain subjects could not be discussed. The inner circle of the family was not a place where young people, or even their parents, could talk easily about personal matters, least of all sex. Parents did not usually speak of sexual matters to their children, not even mother to daughter or father to son. Cross-gender discussion of this topic was even more strongly forbidden.

Anything that even hinted at sexuality was suppressed within the family circle. The people of Chuuk once possessed a long list of polite circumlocutions used for certain parts of the body and their functions as well as other words that might have sexual innuendos. The Ulithi people avoided the direct words for a man's loincloth and the woman's lavalava, referring to them instead by the materials from which they were made. Women's underwear was kept out of sight of the men in the household. Women undergoing menstruation were supposed to keep all visible evidence hidden from the eyes of the men in their family. In many island groups they left the household altogether to spend the duration of their monthly period in a separate menstrual house.

The discretion imposed between brothers and sisters—a relationship that would have included first cousins as well as siblings—was of the strictest kind. Throughout the Central Carolines, boys who had reached puberty were not even permitted to sleep in the same house with their sisters; they were expected to spend the evenings in the canoe house or family meetinghouse where men from the lineage normally gathered to work and relax. On some islands it was regarded as scandalous for a brother and sister to share food or even drink out of the same cup. There was an old-fashioned formality to the relationship between men and women within the Micronesian family that would have made nineteenth-century Victorian standards seem risqué by comparison.

One of the greatest insults an islander can suffer is to hear someone make a sexual reference about his mother or sister, however oblique. Once, in a moment of playfulness, I mentioned to a Micronesian friend of mine how pretty his female cousin was. He didn't go so far as to punch me, although for a moment I thought he would, but he told me to shut up and never say anything like that again. You can imagine the reaction if I had suggested to him that his mother was having an affair with someone, or that a friend of mine had made a successful sexual overture to his sister. Even a vulgar word uttered by someone in the presence of one's sister can initiate a drama, as it did on one memorable occasion when I was teaching at Xavier High School.

The Chuukese boy who had been within earshot when the curse was shouted by another student within hearing of his female cousin went upstairs to the dormitory to brood for an hour before going berserk. He charged into the study hall with a machete in hand prepared to go after the student who had cursed in front of his "sister." The boy had to be wrestled to the ground and disarmed by two older students to avoid further mayhem. If ever I needed proof that the old cross-gender taboos were in force, this was surely it.

But that happened thirty-five years ago. Today, many of these old prohibitions have fallen into disuse. Brothers and sisters, once prohibited from sleeping in the same house, comfortably share quarters in today's modern home, divided into separate rooms. There is not the same worry about concealing women's undergarments that there once was; they are hung on the line to dry in full sight of everyone in the family. Even in those islands where the ban was once observed, brothers and sisters show little reluctance to drink from the same cup or eat from the same plate. But most important of all, mass media have entered the bosom of the family, bringing an element of explicit sexuality that would have scandalized Micronesians in an earlier age. Video rentals are available to anyone who wants them, even in the more remote atolls. While most families exercise discretion in the type of movies they allow to be shown at home, the R-rated movie is becoming standard fare in some households. Even if movies are chosen not because of their sexual content but despite it, the occasional love scenes found in adventure movies become awkward moments when the entire family is grouped around the television set. Brothers and sisters may glance at one another as they try to decide whether to fast-forward through a bedroom scene, or they may just stare at the floor embarrassed that they are in one another's presence.

With the relaxation of taboos within the family, a more casual relationship is developing between brothers and sisters today. Families may seem to adapt to this with relative ease, but there are signs that those sexual transgressions within families that the old respect forms were intended to guard against are becoming a serious issue. Incest was once a rather rare occurrence in the islands, if we can believe the early anthropological studies, but a survey that Micronesian Seminar conducted in four major island groups some years ago turned up over a hundred confirmed cases. I know of several young women who have had to be sent off island to live with relatives because they had been regularly molested by their fathers or uncles. No one has yet proved that the increasing problem of incest is the result of the breakdown of the old respect forms within the Micronesian family, but there are strong hints of a connection between the two.

Even with the attrition of the traditional respect forms within the family, the old rule continues to be observed: no talk of sex within the family. This denies young adolescents in all but the most modernized families someone to confide in about such matters. Marshallese teenagers had a tradition of being able to talk to their grandparents freely about sexual encounters, but in the smaller family household of our day grandparents are often not readily available. To whom do young Micronesians go for counsel on sexual matters? Not usually to student counselors or church pastors. They are bound to feel uncomfortable attending coed sex education classes, especially if there is any chance that a close relative of the opposite sex is in the same class. Yet, some form of sexual counseling and easy access to someone to whom they can speak about sexual matters is today becoming a more urgent need for young islanders, even if the traditional norms continue to impose a barrier to meeting this need. It is tempting to dismiss the old taboos within the family as outdated and needlessly restrictive. On the other hand, the apparent increase in incest as families modernize and begin to discard these taboos suggests caution in ridding the family of these traditional restraints. They might still serve a purpose in today's family.

Nightcrawling and Dating

He had seen her again with her parents in church last Sunday. She was wearing the same green dress that she had on the week before, but had added a different pair of earrings. He thought that she might have noticed him as she was stepping into her pew. He had given her a sidelong glance, the same sort of look that he cast at her when she was standing near the door of the church before the service. He had been too embarrassed to look directly at her, and trying to strike up a conversation was simply out of the question. If only she had a brother, it would be so much easier. All he would have to do was approach the brother to ask him something so that the two of them could get a short conversation going. It would give him an excuse to get within talking range of her, even with her family around her. If he could get her attention for a short time, he might transmit a subtle signal of his fascination with her: a tilt of the head, a glancing look, a cocked eye. But it would have to be subtle so that it wasn't offensive to her family; that would ruin everything.

He thought that she might have noticed his sidelong glance, or perhaps the way in which he hung back at the front of the church earlier, always keeping her within eyesight even if he deliberately looked off in every direction but hers. In any case, he was prepared to take a chance. Late that evening he would make his move. He knew where she lived and even in what part of the house she usually slept. He would slip on dark clothing, quietly make his way to her house, avoiding the main paths, and sneak into her house to ask her if she was willing to come out with him for a while. Soon he would know if she had the same strong feelings for him that he had for her.

The old myth that in the South Seas sexual adventures were open and shame-free has endured over the ages, fed as it is by a rich and fanciful literature in the West. In fact, sexual adventures, even by the young, had to be arranged subtly and conducted in secrecy, as the above account suggests. A young man embarking on a sexual conquest had to do so stealthily to avoid offending the girl's family and publicly violating the cultural standards that governed behavior between the sexes.

Nightcrawling, the strategy adopted by the young man in the vignette above, was once common throughout much of Micronesia. The term for it in the local language is still used today in Chuuk, Pohnpei, and Kosrae, although nightcrawling may now refer to any secret liaison between a young couple regardless where it occurs. In the classical form, the young man would slip into the girl's house in the evening, quietly awaken her from her sleep without disturbing other members of the family, and invite her to join him in a sexual encounter. But there were other ways of setting up an assignation with a girl. A boy might slip a note to his sweetheart, often by means of a third party, inviting her to meet him at some pre-arranged place.

The trick would have been to find a clandestine meeting spot and to make it there and back without attracting the attention of anyone in the village. The beach was sometimes used for this purpose in the small atolls, but the beach could itself become crowded with couples looking for privacy for the same reason. In place of love notes, other means of arranging a tryst could be used. My Xavier students used to regale me with explanations of what message a particular type of flower worn in the ear and tilted in a particular way could convey to a girl who was watching for such a signal.

Dating, as we know it in the West, was unacceptable in traditional island societies. A boy and a girl would come to know one another through casual contact, of course, but this was always as part of a group. For a boy and girl to show any interest in one another openly, much less spend any time together by themselves publicly, was to flout custom. Those who noticed would have simply assumed that they were having an affair. Even the kind of formal courtship that was practiced in the Philippines, with a young man making an appearance at the house of the girl and talking to her in the middle of the family circle, would have been unthinkable in the islands. Such an event would have been reserved, instead, for the end of the "courtship" process, when the young man along with some of his family would show up at the home of his girlfriend to arrange for the traditional marriage.

The island "dating" process, with its opportunities for intimate conversation as well as physical romance, would have had to be conducted in private. The need to keep all this secret over a period of months in a small village would have taxed the ingenuity of any romantically involved couple. In time, of course, others were bound to discover what was going on. For a while, the girl's family might turn a blind eye to what their daughter was doing, especially if they approved of the object of her desire and thought that the relationship would probably end in marriage. If they disapproved of her choice, they might conspire to end the relationship. For all the taboos that surrounded public sexual display, island parents understood that clandestine romance was an essential part of growing up and preparing for marriage. They might publicly feign indignation, but parents themselves had been through the same experiences when they were young and would have been more tolerant than they appeared. Besides, they understood that the sexual experimentation of their adolescent children was one of the few ways in which young people could free themselves, even for a short time, from the strong control of the family and assert themselves as individuals.

There was a shared understanding that once a boy and girl were openly seen in one another's company, they were regarded as betrothed. Throughout the period of romance, even if the boy and girl were meeting secretly every night and the whole village knew of the affair, that did not give them the right to associate with one another publicly. Their relationship may have been sensed but it was not publicly acknowledged. As soon as they began sleeping through the night in the same house or they otherwise signaled to others they were a couple, they were as good as married. There is a whole body of amusing tales describing the lengths to which men might go to avoid being detected after falling asleep with their girlfriend, but there are still other tales of the ruses that families who wanted desirable matches for their daughters might use to get the young man to oversleep. Once maneuvered into this situation, the couple would initiate a meeting of their families to formalize the union, after which they were free to live together as a pair. In most cases, a formal church or civil marriage was merely an afterthought.

Today there is far more openness in the relationship between boys and girls. In the early 1960s on my first visit to Palau, I was surprised to see girls on the back of motorcycles clinging to young men as they roared back from the bars late on a weekend evening. With the lifting of the ban on alcohol that was in force until 1960, bars and nightclubs sprang up everywhere offering drinking and dancing for young patrons. The disco craze in the next decade gave rise to more respectable places, with their strobe lights and live bands. By the end of the 1970s, young women in town no longer had to fear the social stigma of being termed "bar girls" to enjoy an evening out. Western dancing, with boys and girls paired on the floor and even holding one another in their arms, was gaining social acceptance, despite the radical difference from traditional island dancing in which groups of men danced with men and women with women. Dancing and drinking had quickly caught on with young people and soon were generally tolerated by the not so young nearly everywhere in Micronesia.

Nowadays, people who would have once been shocked to see

a young couple in town holding hands in public or eating together on a dinner date probably wouldn't think twice about it. Dating has become acceptable today in the towns, as the old standards governing the public behavior of young men and women have been relaxed. The difference between then and now is not in sexual behavior as such, but in the discretion with which it is carried out. As boys and girls become teenagers in the pattern of the West, nightcrawling is on the way to becoming a lost art.

Sex as a Family Concern

It was an open secret in his family that Carlos was in love. For months now his family had noticed his long absences at night and some had even heard his quiet returns in the early hours of the morning. Uncharacteristically, Carlos was sleeping late into the mornings, long after the rest of the family had finished their coffee and had already begun their daily routine. Even when he was with the family, he would go about his tasks absentmindedly, saying very little to others in the family. And, of course, there were the rumors going around the village that had already reached the ears of those in Carlos' family.

Finally, Carlos gathered his courage to approach his uncle, admit his interest in the girl, and ask if his uncle and the family would speak to the girl's family on his behalf. For the next several days the family was astir over the request: there were hushed conversations between Carlos' uncle and his father, sudden visits from his mother's two older sisters that always turned into long conversations outside the house, quiet discussions between Carlos' mother and father. After three weeks of this low-key drama, Carlos' uncle summoned the boy to tell him that the family had approved his request and arrangements had been made to meet with the girl's family the following Friday.

There was not much chatter among the small party as they approached the house of Carlos' girlfriend. Carlos' mother and father walked with three other older members of the family, some of them carrying cartons filled with island food, while Carlos followed at a distance in vacant-eyed silence. They were greeted warmly by the girl's family and invited inside to take their seats,

Carlos' family on one side of the room and the girl's family on the other. As Carlos sat down on the opposite side of the room from his girlfriend, he noticed her presence but was too timid to do anything more than steal a glance at her every so often. As he dropped his eyes and stared intently at the floor, his uncle cleared his throat and, identifying himself as the spokesman of Carlos's family, began to explain their purpose in paying this visit to the family.

Sexual matters may not have been spoken of within the family, but it was understood that the sexual conduct of its members was a family concern. Room was allowed the young for a certain amount of experimentation in this area since sex was a part of growing up, but the experimentation was not to run wild. In the past, children were cautioned against beginning sexual adventures too early; otherwise, they were told, they would become sick. Young people were also strongly warned not to show any sexual interest in anyone in their own extended family or clan for fear of getting a bad name and discouraging a good match. Sexuality, like other areas of life, was meant to serve the interests of the family.

There are any number of historical examples of this. During the height of the whaling trade in the Micronesia in the mid-nineteenth century, young girls from Pohnpei and Kosrae were brought to the ships, sometimes by their fathers, to provide sexual comfort to the crew of the ships in order to procure trade goods—especially iron tools, clothing, and tobacco—for their families. In Palau and Yap young women were once taken, with the consent of their parents, to work in the men's clubhouses in other villages as sexual attendants. At the end of their service they received some of the island valuables that served as "money" and so brought wealth and social status to their own families upon their return.

Everywhere and at all times, young women were expected to use their natural charms to secure a good marriage, one that would gain their family land and prestige. Accordingly, families might turn a blind eye to the involvement of one of their daughters with an American Seabee or an expatriate lawyer or businessman, especially if there was a good chance that the relationship might end in marriage. While Micronesian parents, like parents everywhere, hoped that their children's marriages might offer their children personal happiness, they never lost sight of the benefits that such marriages could bring the entire family. Marriage might offer personal satisfaction for the couple under the right circumstances, but, whether or not that happened, it should certainly bestow blessings to the families of the couple.

In the past, arranged marriages were the rule nearly everywhere in the islands. The family would exercise strong, although not complete, control over the choice of a mate for one of its sons or daughters. This in itself was not much different from what would have been found in medieval Europe or, for that matter, in many parts of the world even today. Arranged marriages were justified on the understandable assumption that marriage was a good deal more than the formal union of a man and a woman. It was a bond between two different families, and the families would have to maintain a good working relationship between one another if the marriage were to succeed. In traditional Micronesia, of course, there was no question of the couple walking off together to make a life for the two of them and whatever children they produced. Where would they have gone? Even after marriage, they were bound to their blood families as closely as they were to one another. The welfare of their own kin was always an important factor that would have to be balanced against their relationship with one another.

Even in bygone times the arranged marriage was not always definitive. A young couple who were unhappy together might split up after a year or two together, thus sending a clear signal to their families that despite their readiness to submit to the wishes of the families they had clear interests of their own in the matter. When this happened, parents usually learned from the mistake and paid greater heed to their son or daughter's wishes on the choice of a marriage partner the next time around. In more recent years a compromise seems to have been struck between the interests of the couple and those of the families. Today young people normally choose their own partners, but the marriage is still subject to the approval of both families. The boy's family will normally accompany him to the home of his girlfriend to ask her family for her hand. If both families agree to the arrangement, the young pair will leave together to begin to live openly with one another as a married couple. Young people may choose their partners, but parents retain veto power over the arrangement. After all, parents continue to recognize the stake of the family in any marriage, and so must ensure that the family interests are preserved.

With so many young people leaving the islands these days, families are losing even the limited control they once enjoyed over the choice of marriage partners for their children. One island woman I know, while away in college, married a young man attending the same school in Michigan. When they returned to the islands a year or two later, the meeting between the two families to seek permission for marriage was a mere formality. She had a child by that time, and the issue had been decided even before her husband asked for her hand. Sometimes young people don't even bother with this formality. A Micronesian friend of mine once told me that he received a phone call from a young man attending school in California with the request that he inform his parents that he was getting married to a girl from his own island living in the United States. Because the older Micronesian was distantly related to both the boy and the girl, he was supposed to authorize the marriage in lieu of the families. Such cases are becoming ever more common today. As they are, parents are surrendering their veto power over the marriages of their children, the last measure of control they retained over the choice of a marriage partner.

Meanwhile, men are expected to provide benefits for their wife's family, whether in the form of land, hospitality for her relatives, or financial support for family functions. Married women remain today, as they have been in the past, responsible for their blood relatives. We have already seen in Chapter 4 an illustration of what this responsibility might entail for the woman and her husband. Most married couples even today take this responsibility seriously and are prepared to direct their own resources toward their blood kin in time of need, especially on the occasion of a marriage or funeral. Oddly enough, however, women are beginning to block rather than aid their own relatives from access to their husband's resources. I know one older Micronesian woman, married for years to an American, who has taken it upon herself to become the gatekeeper for the family. Any of her relatives who want to stay with the couple must ask her permission, which she does not easily give. Similarly, any requests for money from her kin are more liable to be turned down than approved. She and women like her who shield their spouses from the demands of their own families are possibly the prophets of a new age, one in which marriage increasingly serves the couple and their children rather than the families of the couple, as would have been expected in the past.

Sex in the islands might have once been at the service of the family, but there are strong signs today that, like so many other elements in life, it is being appropriated by the individual.

The Real Power of Women

Appearances Can Be Deceptive

We were on the back of a flatbed truck filled with students when a drunken young man stepped into the middle of the road and tossed a rock at our truck. I hopped off the back of the truck and was running toward him when I was intercepted by a woman in her thirties. She blocked my path with arms outstretched, apologizing all the while for the young man's drunken behavior. She then turned to the young man and led him off, while I stood bewildered by the scene. Meanwhile, the students were beckoning me back onto the truck. Just as I was ready to hop back on, I heard a loud slap as the young man struck the woman who was leading him away from trouble. I must have looked as though I was ready to chase after the drunk because I heard one of the students say, "That's okay, Father. She's the sister of that guy."

As we drove on, at each house we passed we would see women holding toddlers, gathering the small children, or hanging out laundry. Women were everywhere, it seemed, while men were invisible. "Where are all the men?" I asked one of the students. "They're all in the house sleeping or playing cards," he laughingly replied.

A mile or two farther on we reached a bend in the road. As we rounded the bend, I saw two middle-aged men with cigarettes in their mouths enjoying an animated conversation. Trailing behind them by several yards was a woman who could have been the wife of one of the two men. She was staggering under the weight of the large basket she was carrying, the two men

oblivious to her burden. I had only been on the island for a few
months, but I remember thinking as I watched the woman trail
behind the two men: such is the unfortunate fate of women in the
islands.

Like so many other new visitors to the islands, I couldn't help but
feel that Micronesian women were ill-used creatures. Just look at how
they're treated. A young woman tries to intervene to help her drunken
brother, who repays her with blows to the face. Men enjoy themselves
while women struggle with their heavy work burdens. Other images
flash to mind. Sometimes we would see a married couple walking
down the road, the man usually a few steps ahead of his wife, eyes
fixed on the road ahead as if he were deliberately ignoring her. Then
there is my own vivid memory of a man and his wife entering our
school chapel after Sunday mass had already begun. The man plunked
himself down in the last remaining seat on the pew, while his wife took
her place on the floor at the back of the chapel. Chivalry had not died
in Micronesia, I reflected; it had not even been born.

These impressions seem to be confirmed at any major social event
in the islands. While men are seated at feasts, busily feeding themselves, the women are scurrying around refilling platters of food on
the table and tending to the needs of the guests. At the conclusion of
the party the women will be occupied picking up the plates, cleaning
the tables, and dividing up the leftover food. Newcomers may well
ask themselves if there is any work connected with the feast that is *not*
assigned to women. Or, to frame the question more broadly, is the role
of women in island society to play the part of servants so that men
might enjoy themselves in peace?

Not so many years ago the treatment of women became an issue
on the University of Guam campus when one of the teachers noticed
young women in his class dropping to their knees and crawling to
their seats in front of their brothers. This may have been the customary respect behavior young women showed their "brothers" in the
atolls of Micronesia, but it registered as degrading in the eyes of the
American teacher who witnessed it. What the teacher did not know,
of course, is that brothers would have been expected to practice other,
less obvious forms of respect behavior toward their sisters. On their
own island, they might have risen from their seats to allow their sisters

Fig. 10. Palauan woman on her way to work (ca. 1960).
Courtesy of FSM Congress Library.

to pass by without having to crawl. But even if the teacher had known this, he still might have concluded that the forms of respect required of women are more demeaning than those practiced by men.

All the signs seem to point to the same conclusion: women appear to be downtrodden creatures who are regarded by males, and perhaps even by themselves, as inferior beings. For women to be denied equality with men is understandable perhaps. After all, this has been the case in the West for centuries; only recently has there been any serious attempt to correct this imbalance. Yet the status of island women, who seemingly must assume a servile stance and bear any punishment meted out by men, is something of a different order altogether. In the eyes of a westerner, this is a wrong that screams to the heavens for redress.

Appearances can be deceptive, especially in another culture. The deferential public behavior of women toward men is far from defining their importance in the islands. Outward appearances to the contrary, women have always enjoyed authority and respect in the island cultures of Micronesia. But why wouldn't they? In a traditional seafaring society in which men might be voyaging for long periods of time and sometimes never return, women were the keepers of the home— and, most importantly, the land. It is no exaggeration to state that in the matrilineal society of the islands the social edifice was built on the foundation of women. Women were the custodians of the land, the anchor of the family, providing continuity in the home and the community.

My own first impressions, recorded in the vignette at the beginning of this chapter, have been replaced over the years by a more informed appraisal of the status of women in the islands. It is impossible to watch husbands and wives interact with one another without coming to an appreciation of how strong the understated importance of the wife truly is in the home. The man of the household may claim to be the "head of the family," but in actual fact he will defer to his wife's wishes repeatedly. What school the children attend, how the holidays will be spent, how much money will be sent to needy relatives—all such questions are decided as much by the woman of the household as by the man. This should be no surprise to westerners, who probably experience much the same in their own families. "She who is to be obeyed" is my brother's code name for his wife; many Micronesian men could say much the same.

The woman's respected place in the family is not just owing to the effect of modernization on the island family. The Micronesian woman in the past, linked as she was with her blood relatives, would have had an even stronger influence in the family. She and her lineage, after all, were compared to the "hull of the canoe" in the old metaphors, while her husband was seen as the "outrigger." His role was to steady the vehicle; hers, with the help of her blood relatives, was to bear its load and maintain its course. Her feelings on family matters may not always have been voiced directly, but they were registered strongly just the same. As always, her influence had to be gauged not simply by her own words, but by the words coming from the mouths of male relatives over which she exerted a strong influence.

"I was brought up to feel important as a woman," a well-educated Chuukese friend of mine once remarked. Her sentiments would be echoed by Palauan and Marshallese women, as well as by women in the other island cultures of Micronesia. She was expressing something that I failed to recognize for a long time, just as it eludes many visitors to the islands today. Whatever the outward appearances, women have always held a respected place in island society. The public image of women may seem old-fashioned, terribly out of date for westerners who have been raised to revere the feminist agenda of the last forty or fifty years. But forcing such an agenda on an evolving island society, one with its own patterns of behavior, could be counterproductive in the end. First, we might take the time to look beyond the appearances and come to an appreciation of what women's role in island life has been and continues to be today.

Women's Work

The woman rose with the sun and glanced anxiously at the clock before bolting from her bed. It was already six o'clock and she had plenty of things to do before leaving for work in the office. She turned toward her husband, who was still sound asleep, dressed as quietly as she could, and left to check on her children. She gently woke them up and whispered to them that it was time for them to get ready for school. When she was satisfied that they were all awake, she hurried into the kitchen to boil water for coffee and check to see that there was enough food for breakfast. She then dashed out into the yard, picking up a rake as she left the house to clean up outside. When she finished that, she hurried into the house again to begin tidying up the living room. She picked up schoolbooks and put them in their proper place and then started collecting discarded clothes to put in the clothes washer. Before she had a chance to catch her breath, it was time for her to check on breakfast. She put on the table a loaf of bread and some leftovers from the evening meal, made sure that the water had been boiled, and set out a stack of dishes that her family could use for breakfast.

Slowly the children, still rubbing their sleepy eyes, filed in for breakfast. She poured them their milk, warmed up the food from the evening before, and got them settled at the table, just as her husband appeared in the kitchen. As he slumped into his chair with a magazine in his hand, she poured his coffee and then turned to her children to make sure they had eaten. Within a minute or two, she was back in the living room making sure that her children had their schoolbooks before she hustled them out the door so they wouldn't be late. Then she checked on the laundry again before she finally made a cup of coffee for herself and sat down with a sigh of relief. But the satisfaction didn't last long. As she looked at her watch, she jumped back up with a start; she only had five minutes to change and get ready for her ride to the office. Back to the bedroom she darted before reappearing minutes later with her purse in her hand. It was time for her to get to work.

A woman's work seemingly never ends. Or does it? The vignette presented above was the opening scene in a video drama that Micronesian Seminar produced on women's work today. Island women these days seem to be charged with doing just about everything in the home: they take care of the children, prepare the food, do the laundry, keep the house clean, and do their husband's bidding. Then, on top of all that, many women hold down a full-time job in an office. Island men, on the other hand, seem to enjoy a leisurely existence: they may have to show up at an office during the week, but their other responsibilities seem modest by comparison. Men often jump into a boat to go out fishing for the family—something that is almost recreational—and they may engage in modest cultivation on some islands or breadfruit harvesting on others. But these are manageable tasks if not always enjoyable ones. It is women who seem to be burdened with the management of the family and the home.

It wasn't always this way. In the past a sharp distinction was made between men's work and women's work, with the labor rather equally apportioned out to the two genders. Men were associated with the sea, so they were responsible for construction and maintenance of canoes and for all deep-sea fishing. Women, on the other hand, did inshore fishing and gathered seafood in many of the island societies. Men were entrusted with the care of trees: besides planting and picking coconut and breadfruit trees, they felled trees, carved timber, and built houses. Women, for their part, were usually tasked with the cultivation of the land and the production of staple food crops. Men might have been engaged in village meetings and other public activities at which participation was required in order to maintain the standing of their family. Women, however, made their own contribution to the prestige of the family by manufacturing traditional valuables such as loom-woven lavalavas, pandanus mats, medicine, and ornaments. These valuables were used to purchase canoes and were given as gifts at weddings, funerals, and other significant community events. Even in the care of the adolescent children, responsibility was split along gender lines, with the men assuming care of the boys and women providing guidance for the girls.

The dividing line between men's work and women's work might shift a bit from island to island: taro cultivation, for instance, was done by men in Chuuk and the Marshalls, but by women in Palau and Yap. Even so, the principle of division of labor was honored everywhere. There was men's work and there was women's work, and never would the two overlap. The work assigned to men and women might be different, but each was regarded as integral to the welfare of the whole community.

The principle of complementarity was honored even when the community gathered to work together on a joint project. In preparation for the replacement of the thatch on a meetinghouse, for instance, men would gather the leaves to be used for the roofing, the women would plait the thatch, the men climbed the rafters to attach the pieces of thatch to the roof, and the women would prepare the food for lunch. Even in something as commonplace as breadfruit preparation in Chuuk, the same kind of division of labor was employed. The men would pick the breadfruit and carry it to the cookhouse, where the women would scrape off the skin and cook it. The men would then pound the breadfruit chunks and shape it into loaves, after which the women would wrap the loaves in breadfruit leaves and store them.

A division of labor so finely delineated demanded good coor-

dination between men and women. Men in the outer islands, for
instance, were expected to let the women know what sort of fishing
they intended to do so that the women could prepare the right kind
of cooked food to accompany the fish at the community celebration
when the men returned. The interplay of gender roles contributed
greatly to the feeling that everything done within the community was
the product of all. This satisfaction, in turn, was the groundwork for
a genuine community spirit.

The old balance of labor by gender has been upset by changes
in island society. Women's work roles have been altered because the
food crops women once produced have been replaced with imported
food in many parts of Micronesia. Locally grown taro, breadfruit, and
bananas have been replaced by rice, bread, ramen, and other foreign
foodstuffs. The declining importance of crop cultivation, at least in the
towns, and modern kitchen appliances would seem to have cut down
the burden assigned to women. By the same token, much of the traditional workload of men has also disappeared: canoes are no longer
made in most places, house construction is increasingly contracted out
to specialists, men are no longer forced to make their own rope, and
many of the heavier tasks that men once assumed in food production
are no longer practiced. In lieu of all these traditional work roles, men
have been turning to full-time wage employment for decades now.

Yet, the impact of these changes has greatly changed the balance
of the workload shouldered by women. As rice increasingly replaces
breadfruit or taro as the main staple in the island diet, men's role
in the preparation of food greatly diminishes. In Chuuk, most of the
work in the production of breadfruit was done by men: they picked
the breadfruit, prepared the cook fire, pounded the breadfruit after
it was cooked, and buried some of it in pits to preserve it for future
meals. With the elimination of all this hard work, formerly done by
men, all of the food preparation can be readily turned over to women.
As cooking becomes easier, the entire "kitchen" is being turned over
to women.

Women, too, are assuming a more prominent role in child care, as
the breakdown of the extended family strips them of the adults they
once could depend on for help. The relatives who might have once
served as surrogate parents are no longer present to help in the nuclear
family of today's society. Meanwhile, women are expected to not

only take care of the younger children, but also look after older children well into their adolescent years as they continue their education through high school and sometimes longer. With most of their children in school, moreover, they can no longer count on turning their younger children over to the supervision of elder siblings, as they once did.

The vignette with which this section began, then, is an illustration of the imbalanced workload resulting from social change. Household tasks and other work within the family may have been equitably shared in the past, but this is often no longer the case today. Even though modern conveniences have made household work easier, much more of it than ever before seems to fall to women.

The distribution of work may have changed, but the underlying principle of the division of labor into men's work and women's work persists. I saw that clearly some years ago at Xavier High School, where the male boarding students were required to do their own laundry. Because washing clothes was so strongly associated with women's work, much more so than cooking or housecleaning, the boys vied with one another in an attempt to find in the local community promised sisters—girls whom they could treat like real sisters. When a boy had found one, he would be seen carrying his dirty clothes to the house of his new "sister," thus avoiding the opprobrium of doing women's work.

Old patterns of thought die a slow death, as we have noted before, even when the practices supporting them change. The imbalance in the workload of women is being addressed today, but only in the most modernized of Micronesian families. In some families, where both the husband and wife have full-time wage employment, the men are beginning to assume some of the housekeeping work and are even taking on some of the child care responsibilities. But such families remain the rare exception to the old general rule governing division of labor.

Wage jobs in the modern sector were at first treated as men's work, but everywhere in the islands women are gaining access to a greater share of these positions. The feeling that women were intruding into a sphere of activity that properly belonged to men seems to have abated. Still, there is persistent resentment by subordinate male employees toward women holding positions of authority in the office. The men may not express this resentment openly, but the indirect signs are unmistakable: assignments are deliberately put off and appointments to meet with the woman in charge not kept. Micronesian women may have gained access to jobs in the modern sector, but not to the full spectrum of jobs, especially those at the top.

The campaign for equal rights for women is being taken up by educated women with the support of international organizations, but the term "rights" has little resonance in Micronesia, as we have already seen. Open access to wage employment and the authority that accompanies it assumes the readiness of island people to tear down the great divide between gender roles, something that has been a long-standing organizational principle in Micronesian societies. Inroads have been made in recent decades, but resistance to the breakdown of old organizational patterns persists. With the elimination of the traditional division of labor, many Micronesians fear that the easy collaboration of men and women in the past may yield to open competition between the genders.

Power behind the Scenes

The women's group gathered for their monthly meeting in the office of an international organization. They seemed oddly unenthusiastic, perhaps a bit discouraged, as they took their places around a large table. Gina, a newly elected member of the state legislature and its only female member, spoke first. When some of the other women around the table congratulated her for her recent victory at the polls, she smiled wanly before she went on to describe her frustrations. She had hoped to be appointed to one or two of the committees, she told the group, because of her long experience in health and education matters. Although she had made known her willingness to serve, she found her name on none of the new committees when the lists appeared a month or two after the elections. One of the other women, in an effort to cheer up her friend, suggested that she could at least make her voice heard on these matters from the floor of the legislature. Gina shook her head sadly as she turned in the direction of her friend and told her that she didn't think she was going to get much of a hearing. She explained that whenever she turned on her microphone to speak during a session, a number of the other legislators would stand and leave the chamber as if they all had to head to the men's room. Others would flip off their microphones, lean over to those alongside them and engage them in conversation while Gina was trying to make a statement.

Most of the other women around the table nodded sympathetically. One started to rattle off some of the problems she was having as director of a state government department. Men who formerly had been known for their prompt submission of reports no longer seemed capable of getting in their paperwork on time, even her closest friends in the department would excuse themselves from meetings, and her smile was often met with vacant stares when she circulated among her staff. Her story prompted others to launch into their own recital of woes. Finally, one of the women at the table asked the question: "What can we do to assure the men we work with that we want to be partners, not competitors for power?" There were no answers to that question.

Where are the women decision makers, females with authority in the modern island government? There may be a very few, as the vignette above suggests, but their number is far from what might be expected if women's leadership role were equal to men's. In today's modern island government men continue to occupy nearly all the leadership positions, not just in elected office but as department heads and key aides to senior officials. The main legislative bodies in Micronesia—the national congresses of Palau, the Marshalls, and the Federated States of Micronesia—have only three women out of a combined total of seventy-six members. Women, then, comprise a mere four percent of the total representatives in these law-making bodies. Moreover, when the occasional woman does get elected or appointed to a leadership position, she faces the difficulties described above.

The general absence of women from these public leadership positions can be traced back to the principle of division of labor in the islands discussed earlier in this chapter. Men do one type of work; women do another. An important corollary of that principle relates to the distribution of authority in Micronesian societies: men take the public decision-making roles, while women exercise their authority behind the scenes. Men are the overt leaders, standing front and center as they make speeches in which decisions are presented to the public. Women, on the other hand, convene behind the curtains when they discuss family or community matters but almost never publicly present the results of the considerable influence they hold. We enlightened outsiders might judge this reprehensible in this age of gender equality, but this was the formula that Micronesian societies lived by for ages.

It would be a mistake to think that because men always assumed the more dominant position, women were relatively powerless in traditional Micronesian societies. Women shared in the exercise of power, even if much of this power was subtly exercised. The authority of women in island society has always been rooted in the traditional roles that were enjoyed by women. They were seen as the guardians of the land, the keepers of the peace, and important counselors on family and community matters.

As guardians of the land, women had a strong say over the disposal of family property and, according to the rules of a matrilineal society, were expected to pass on this land from one generation to another through their daughters. In some islands, the senior women of the lineage had the power to decide who would have the use of what piece of land. If someone in the family wanted to give away a land parcel as restitution for a misdeed or a reward for a service rendered, he was required to get the approval of his sisters before doing so. Even in Yap, where power was famously skewed toward males, the sister of the head of a family could disinherit her nephews for failure to carry out their responsibility. In effect, the women of the family held veto rights over the disposal of land, even if they were not the ones to announce such decisions to those affected.

Women were also peacemakers. Their peace-making role meant that they could do much more than plead that warfare or other hostilities be stopped. They had the power to force men to make peace, especially in village conflicts when older women were present. Women from both sides often met together to arrange the terms of peace, later informing the males of their family what these terms would be. This role continues even to the present day, long after warfare between villages or islands has ended. The young woman who tried to stop me from tackling her drunken brother after he had thrown a stone at our truck was fulfilling this role. In many islands, the mere appearance of an older woman is enough to end a village or family brawl.

Women's exercise of authority in family or community matters took many forms. In the neighboring atolls of Yap, if women felt that

Fig. 11. Older Palauan woman weaving while minding the children (1953).
Courtesy of FSM Congress Library.

the men were neglecting their duties, they might gather at the house of the island chief to demand an end to the *tuba* (fermented coconut sap) drinking sessions that normally went long into the evening. The chief would accordingly announce a ban on *tuba* that might last for weeks or even months. In Palau it was the women of the lineage who met to choose their own lineage leader, who by virtue of his title might also become the village chief. If the women were not satisfied with his performance, they could depose him and choose a replacement. Throughout the islands in general, no lineage leader would dare make an important decision without first consulting his sisters for fear that the decision would later have to be revoked. Women's power in the family, and by way of the family into the community, might have been indirect, but it was very real.

Power was shared by men and women in traditional Micronesian societies, as we can see. It was governed, of course, by the principle of complementary roles that has always held sway in island cultures: "If the men are doing it, the women shouldn't be doing it." The great divide that separates men's work from women's also distinguishes the way in which men exercise authority from the way in which women do so. It is this "separation of powers" that discourages women from taking public office and acting as spokespersons in the community.

What makes us think that this sacred principle governing division of roles will not erode, as so many other cultural patterns do, in the course of modernization? There are signs that this is happening as the pleas for gender equality intensify and the demands for more women in public decision-making roles grow louder. In one of the state legislatures in the region a bill has already been introduced to allot to women a certain number of seats, and similar measures will certainly follow elsewhere. Still, the tenacity of the principle of gender roles, illustrated in the vignette at the beginning of this section, shows how difficult it will be to break down this barrier. Beyond this, there is the danger of eliminating a system that offered women a limited but protected share in decision making in favor of a modern system that offers possible gains in authority without the cover from men. In a word, there is always the risk that the attempts to empower women, to offer them naked avenues of authority, might have just the opposite effect. Well-intentioned but misinformed efforts to assist women in gaining their rightful place in society could result in the denying them the authority they already enjoy.

Love and Its Expression

Home-Grown Love

*Florencio sat on the edge of his porch with an infant in his
hands and a look of deep satisfaction on his face. The child he
was holding was his own, only a few months old. Florencio's
three older children joined their father on the porch and watched
him almost enviously as he held the infant in the air, shook it
gently, and then quickly pulled the infant toward him. As he
drew the infant toward him, Florencio would sniff all around
the tiny body as he mumbled tender little words to his child.
Then he would extend the infant at arm's length once again,
tilting him this way and that, as he maintained a steady stream
of sweet speech to the child. Occasionally the other children
would gather around the infant and try to play with the newest
member of their family, but their father would just wave them
back. When Florencio's ten-year-old daughter asked to hold
the child for a while, Florencio wordlessly glowered at her. She
could play with the infant later when her mother returned; he
was having too much fun right now to share the infant with his
daughter.*

*Then Florencio heard his young son speak from the other
side of the porch. "Papa, when are you going to help me with my
math homework for tomorrow? You said that we could do it this
afternoon." Florencio glanced at his son and then quickly turned
away, all the while mumbling words to his infant that the child
could not possibly understand.*

Micronesian parents can be very demonstrative in their affection toward infants. They playfully coddle them and kiss them, whispering sweet words, and then pass them over to their spouses, all the while lavishing their full attention on them. In other words, they behave the way parents anywhere in the world might toward a young infant born into their family.

But this doesn't last long. As soon as a new child arrives, the attention given to the slightly older infant abruptly ceases and is refocused on the latest arrival. The child who had once been the center of attention is suddenly demoted and shunted off to the care of an older sibling. This was bound to be traumatic for the child, western-trained psychologists who observed this pattern in the 1950s concluded. The sudden shift from center stage to the far wings would make the child confused and mistrustful of the support of those closest to him. The child's emotional life was certain to be constricted, the social scientists surmised, leaving the child with an impaired sense of trust and a diminished capacity for love.

It was only a matter of time before this theory was discredited. The small child had not been ruined, after all. It had simply been treated to its first lesson in island life: the individual may claim the attention of all for a time, but in the end he or she must yield to the interests of the family. The corollary to this, which the child will eventually learn, is that the family will provide a source of love that will never fail.

As children grew up they were not always treated to the displays of affection that western children might have expected. Generous praise was not heaped on them for every little step forward they took, and positive reinforcement would have been scarce in most island households. Many parents simply expected children to do what they were asked to do, and do it well, without the benefit of the encouraging remarks that western parents might make. A Micronesian adult, speaking about his own boyhood at a public forum some years ago, said that he and his brothers learned to accept the absence of criticism as the highest praise they would receive from their parents. Compliments were rare in his family, he recalled, but he and his siblings had learned to expect few.

Years ago I used to marvel at how dismissive Micronesian parents could be toward their own children. I would often hear parents talking down their children in public, spinning out long lists of negative traits

Fig. 12. Kosraean father and his son (1972). Courtesy of Trust Territory Archives, University of Hawai'i.

that they attributed to them. Their children were stupid and lazy, care-less in their chores at home, disrespectful and ill-mannered, and—as if all this were not enough—ugly besides. Sometimes, the children bore nicknames like "Monkey" or "Frog" or "Goatfish" just to make sure that others didn't miss their physical resemblance to certain members of the animal kingdom. It seemed that physical limitations more often inspired teasing than sympathetic hugs from parents, who did not seem to regard their children's oddities as out-of-bounds. Like those older psychologists with their theories of early emotional damage, I used to wonder what impact all this would have on the fragile egos of Micro-nesian children. In retrospect, I see that I was badly underestimating the ego strength of these children, even as I was accepting at face value the remarks that parents were making about their own children.

What I and others understood as an endless series of putdowns of children by their parents continued into early adulthood. A Palauan woman, a personal friend of mine, once recounted for me what hap-pened when a man showed up at her family's house many years earlier to ask for the hand of her older sister in marriage. As her older sister sat with bowed head, her mother offered a full shopping list of her daughter's faults: she was dull-witted, not very energetic, hardly a rav-ing beauty, and was sure to prove a liability to anyone who wanted to take her in marriage. As she was recounting the story, the woman laughed at how embarrassed she had been for her older sister at the time. But she laughed again at how she had misinterpreted her moth-er's remarks. What she had long since come to recognize was that no mother in those days could have praised her own daughter outside the family any more than a man could have lavished praised on the food he was serving a guest. Words spoken to an outsider about a son or daughter were a formality, and it was just as bad form to speak well of the fruit of your womb as the work of your hands.

Disparaging remarks like those island parents publicly make may not be countenanced in U.S. counseling circles, but they can be viewed through an altogether different lens, as testimony of the tight bond between parent and child. The young person is such an intimate part of the family that he cannot be extolled in public by others in the fam-ily. Self-deprecation is a large part of island style, and nowhere does it come into play more than when a parent refers to his or her own children.

The Micronesian child may not have been offered warm hugs and encouraging words, but the child was offered a secure place in the family. This meant the embrace of a close group that would "feed" the individual, with all that word implied. The family would provide unconditional support, material and emotional, whenever the individual needed it and for as long as it was required. The family was a nest to which the individual could always return. No matter what failures a person has endured, how much he's disappointed others, what a wreck he's made of his life, he knows that he will always be welcomed back into his family. When all else fails, the family remains—traditionally the matrilineage, but increasingly today the nuclear family. Here, above all, was where love was to be found by the Micronesian.

American children with a difficult childhood or a setback with their family sometimes drift off, severing all contact and making their own way through life. We've all met individuals who have resorted to this path. But I know of no Micronesian, however difficult his childhood might have been, who has left his family and struck out on his own without so much as a glance over his shoulder. It is unimaginable for an islander to do so because of all that his family, even a dysfunctional one, means to him—how it defines him, constitutes his identity, and protects him. Going it alone is simply not an option for a Micronesian.

The importance of the family is best illustrated in the poignant story of a young Yapese teenager who was evicted from his father's estate after repeated wrongdoing. In Yap, as in Palau, a young man must live up to the expectations of his father's family to keep his place there, but when all else fails he can find refuge with his mother's family—his matrilineage. Hence, when this young man was turned out, he went back to his mother's lineage, the final resort for someone like him. As it turned out, however, he was also rejected by his mother's family and was asked to move on. Within a day or two, the young man took his own life. What is there to live for when one's own family, and the love that should be found there, fails one?

Displays of Affection

The airport waiting area was unusually crowded that day as I entered to pick up a visitor. It was easy to tell why. Near the

*entrance to the departure lounge stood a middle-aged woman
with a younger woman, perhaps in her late twenties. It was easy
to see that they were the ones who were departing. Both were
smothered by the garlands draped around their necks, and both
were dressed in similar island-style dresses—the high-waisted type
with an embroidered hem—of the same color and pattern. They
had to be mother and daughter, both leaving the island on the
same flight, I concluded. When I asked someone about them, I
was told that the older woman was flying to Hawai'i for medical
referral and could be gone for an indefinite period of time. Her
daughter was accompanying her to watch over her during her
stay.*

*As I watched, well-wishers would occasionally come up and
bid them farewell. Some of the older women in the crowd would
approach them with tears in their eyes, embracing them for a
short time before releasing them and wiping their eyes. But many
of the younger girls seemed far less affected by the departure.
They would come up and kiss them on the cheek, or perhaps
hold both of their hands briefly as they took their leave. The men,
older and younger, appeared more diffident. Most extended their
hand to offer a short handshake before they faded away into the
crowd. Their heads were often bowed and their faces sometimes
betrayed their feelings, but their eyes were dry, I noticed. A few
women spent a noticeably longer period of time saying their
good-byes. They would chat with the two travelers for a bit,
even joke with them to judge from the smiles and quiet laughter
as they talked, and then give them a long embrace.*

*Off to the side a ways stood two men—the husbands of the
two women leaving for Hawai'i, I was told. They seemed so
forgotten, off by themselves, but they were apparently content
to allow the rest of the friends and family to bid their good-byes
to their spouses while they waited for their own chance to wish
them a quiet farewell.*

To an outside observer there are very few displays of affection in
the island family. There are few hugs or kisses exchanged within the
family, and none between family members of opposite sex. To judge
from appearances, the emotional distance between a child and his close

relatives only seemed to increase as the boy or girl grew older. The suppressed expression of affection, of course, is owing to the respect behavior that has already been discussed in Chapter 7. Younger brothers were expected to show deference to older brothers as they matured. Brothers and sisters were supposed to keep their distance from one another as they approached adolescence. Easy familiarity was at odds with the respect behavior the young were supposed to exhibit. Expression of affection, whether within the family or publicly, was governed by cultural norms. The absence of hugs and kisses did not mean that genuine affection was absent, only that island culture dictated that this affection be expressed differently. Island culture shaped the way that love might be demonstrated in public.

Departures, like those described in the vignette above, are often the occasion for emotional expression in the islands. Such departures can be painful experiences, especially when a young person is heading off to school or a patient is bound for medical referral off island. The person leaving is surrounded by family and friends, often wearing a stack of flower leis around his neck or on his head presented by those close to him. There are some hugs, of course, but the most telling demonstrations of affection are the bowed heads of those surrounding the individual, many with eyes misting over. There is no wailing and not many verbal expressions of love, but the way in which friends or family members clasp the hand of the traveler as if reluctant to let go always seemed to me to be a much more genuine gauge of the depth of feeling at such events.

Micronesian funerals, culturally orchestrated in their emotional display, are another case in point. During my earliest years in the islands, I recall being perplexed by the funerals I attended. The keening that was still practiced in those days—and still is in some islands—was bone-chilling as I would approach the house where the body was laid out. The women, usually dressed in black, were gathered around the corpse. Some of them might be crying quietly as they sat on the floor, while others would shuffle over to the casket and break out into tears as they placed an arm on the head of the casket. From time to time a loud, shrill wail would break out and be taken up by everyone in the room. I remember wondering whether these women, who could seemingly turn their grief on or off at will, were hired mourners, or whether their sobs and shrieks were expressions of genuine emotion.

Meanwhile, the men, who were usually nursing a cup of coffee outside at the outer fringes of the wake, maintained the same mask of indifference as always. Even though tears didn't come easily for men in my own culture either, I couldn't help wondering whether these stony-faced island men had any feelings at all.

The display of affection toward the dead person that I was witnessing was culturally determined. It could be exaggerated in the case of women, who sat around the casket weeping loudly and almost throwing themselves on the bier. It might be muted in the case of men, who stood around outside the house with coffee cups in hand chatting among themselves. An observer like myself might have trouble telling how closely a mourner was related to the deceased and how deeply he had been affected by the loss, so culturally patterned were the emotional responses.

For the most part, love was expressed in a matter-of-fact way in normal island life. Adults were ready to provide food for one another and to assist their neighbors in need. Brothers took care of their married sisters, while sisters protected their brothers, intervening when necessary to keep them out of harm's way. While there were no warm signs of affection exchanged between them, for that would have been unseemly, the ways in which they watched out for one another left no doubt that they were not just going through the motions to fulfill a family duty. At no time was this more clearly dramatized than when the family took care of one of its sick members. Many times when I was called to the hospital to pray over a sick person, I would have to push my way through a dozen or so people to get to the bedside. The worried looks on the faces of those gathered around the bedside and the questions they would ask about the condition of the sick person and chances for recovery were more than enough evidence that they were not just there because they had to be. I always left with the assurance that genuine affection was not at all stifled among these people, no matter how stoic and otherwise undemonstrative they might appear.

There are other relationships, too, in which genuine affection may be more openly displayed. Take, for example, the friendship between two young adults of the same sex. When I first arrived in Micronesia I often saw a pair of teenage boys walking hand in hand, their joined hands swinging loosely as with little children. Whenever a student would take my own hand as we walked off the campus toward town, I would instinctively pull back in shame. It just wasn't the kind of thing we westerners felt comfortable doing, at least until we had overcome our initial reactions against such a gesture. In time, however, we came to realize that if those boys holding hands had been gay couples with a mutual sexual attraction, they would *not* have been showing such open affection toward one another.

One of the strongest bonds is the relationship between two promised brothers or sisters. Young men or women who have known one another well will often form a special kind of relationship between them—a sibling bond between two friends who pledge that they will treat one another as brothers or sisters. Unlike real siblings, though, they have no hesitation in spending time together because respect avoidance between them is not a factor. They feel free in calling on one another for help or in confiding to one another. This is as openly warm a relationship as can be found in Micronesia. But why shouldn't it be? These "brothers" or "sisters" have chosen one another, as they could not choose their blood siblings, and can feel entirely comfortable in one another's presence.

Micronesians might not always express their affection as openly as westerners, but the affection is real and runs deep. The display of emotion is culturally controlled, as it is in our own societies, but it can be seen if we know where to look and what signs might betray people's feelings. Anyone who has spent even a short time in the islands can testify to this from personal experience.

Love in Marriage

The announcement was made over the airport speaker system for all departing passengers to proceed to the departure lounge. The two women who were leaving on the flight, a mother and her daughter, perked up at the announcement and made a move toward the immigration counter. The crowd of well-wishers swarming around them pulled back a bit to let them pass. Some of the friends and family were waving handkerchiefs, some had tears in their eyes, but all extended their hands one final time to offer their good-byes. As the crowd parted, the husbands of the two women came forward to say farewell. The older one put his hand briefly on his wife's shoulder and said something to her, his eyes fixed on someone else and his jaw tight. The younger man took the hand of his wife for an instant and pumped it once as he made a humorous remark before he let his arm fall to his side. Then they turned and walked away without so much as glance back as they headed for the parking lot.

Once in the car, the two of them began a stream of forced banter with one another. Whenever there was a pause in the conversation, one of them would begin to chatter about something that had happened to him earlier in the day. It was if they had made a pact to avoid silence at all costs. Finally, when they reached the older man's house, he slowly got out of the car and trudged to the door. Just inside he found a Bible lying on the table. The man picked it up and examined it, let out a long sigh, and made a mental note to tell his wife that she had forgotten her Bible.

Later that evening, the younger man was out with four friends for a few drinks. The conversation had been exceptionally lively until the young man suddenly fell silent and looked away from the circle for a moment or two. Within a split second the teasing began: "Are you missing someone, Lucas? We can get you to the airport for the next flight to Hawai'i." One of his friends started strumming an imaginary guitar and singing "Are You Lonely Tonight?" Snapping out of his revery, Lucas forced a smile and ordered another round of drinks. Then he cheerfully replied: "What do you mean lonely? Now I'm free."

When I first came to Micronesia I was baffled by the relationship between island men and their wives. In the first place, it was difficult to tell who was married to whom; spouses never gave the slightest hint that there was any bond between them. You could be with a group of men and women all day and still not be able to pair them off by the end of that time. Seldom did I see so much as a gentle touch or a reassuring glance pass between a husband and wife. The truth is that they seemed more comfortable when they were at a safe distance from one another. Wives usually walked a step or two behind their husbands and behaved deferentially toward them. At parties, the wife would join the other women flitting from one little task to another while the men relaxed in one another's company somewhere else, usually as far away from the women as possible. It was hard to avoid forming the conclusion that wives were little more than a functional necessity: they were there simply to take care of the kids they bore, keep the house clean, and prepare the food.

I had expected to see the small signs of affection between couples that might be found in my own country: the arm draped around the shoulder, the whispered aside at a public gathering, the embrace at the airport at the departure or arrival of one of them, the little gestures that spoke of the bond between them. Slowly I came to realize that the small signs of intimacy that I had come to assume were indications of a love relationship weren't to be found in the islands. Once again, public display of affection, this time between spouses, was discouraged by culture. What that entailed was not only a set of social regulations, but public ridicule for those people who were brazen enough to transgress. A young friend once admitted to me that he enjoyed driving around town on weekends with his wife at his side, but that he had to think twice about it because of the feedback he was getting from others. His male friends were teasing him about being chained to his wife and being dragged around by her. His wife, in their view, had not only tamed him but had turned him into something less than the man he should have been.

Gradually I learned that there were other ways to take the measure of the relationship between spouses. Once when staying in a village to pick up some of the local language, I couldn't help but hear the pillow talk between a man and his wife who were quartered in the next room, separated from mine by a thin sheet of plywood. Although I couldn't understand much of what was being said in the local language, there was no mistaking the intimacy signaled in the voice inflection. On another occasion, I was sitting at a table with a group of a dozen men enjoying drinks and a lively conversation, when one of the men at the table turned to the bar as his wife picked up the microphone and began a karaoke song. Men out drinking and talking, interrupted by a wife's loud singing? I expected the worst, but was treated to the best. The husband, possessed of a loud voice himself and a little drunk by this time, lowered his voice and gently asked his wife if she could just turn down the volume a notch so that the singing wouldn't bother his friends. I may have feared a harsh scolding, but I should have known better. All of us had often enough witnessed the subtle signs of a warm relationship between a couple—the kind of signs that were transmitted even across public space on that occasion.

In the absence of more dramatic signs of affection, people like me learn to seek other hints. When I was called to a house to care for a sick man or woman, the worried look on the spouse's face was eloquent testimony of the concern and affection felt for the sick partner. The interplay between couples I knew well was especially convincing. At a dinner party at the home of one such couple, I was struck by how often one of the spouses could come to the rescue of the other in an embarrassing situation—when a name was forgotten, a welcome speech temporarily halted, or a gaffe committed. Eventually it became clear to me that the spouses were doing just what they would have been expected to do anywhere: fill in for each other and complete that larger unit that was always envisioned in marriage.

Every now and then there was a more dramatic, almost counter-cultural display of the love between the couple. Once, not too many years ago, I was called to the hospital to provide the last sacraments for a woman who was in severe pain and said to be close to death. When I arrived at her room, I was surprised to find her husband lying on her bed cradling her in his arms as he rocked her gently to ease her pain. This touching scene was an expression of tenderness that I never expected to see in Micronesia, with its taboos on the public expression of marital affection. Upon further reflection, however, I came to realize that over the years I had been treated to far more subtle displays of love that was no less genuine than what I saw in that hospital room. It was all in knowing where to look for the signs.

This is not to re-propagate the old myth of the Blessed Isles in which love reigns unchallenged. There are the usual betrayals of spouses, the heartbreak brought on by affairs, and the stubborn refusals to reconcile. My line of work makes me very aware of all this. But there is also the unmistakable loneliness of one spouse for the other when the two have been separated for a time. I once asked a Yapese friend of mine why Micronesian men who are away from home always seem to talk about missing their children, but never their wives. He popped another betel nut into his mouth, smiled, and in enigmatic Yapese fashion told me that when they *say* they miss their children they *mean* they miss their wives. It just wouldn't be proper for a Micronesian man to admit that he longed to be back with his wife.

These Micronesian couples may barely exchange a word with one another in public and almost never walk side by side, but I've known hundreds of them who had an affection for one another so deep and lasting that even the dismissive social scientists I once read so assiduously in my early years would have had to call it love.

Coping with Conflict

Avoiding Clashes

The fourteen-year-old boy had been at Xavier High School for only a few months, but he seemed especially mature for his years. He was bright, near the top of his class, and was well respected by his classmates. As we sat chatting in my office one day, he casually mentioned that some of his clothes were missing. When I asked him what exactly was missing, he said that he had lost a shirt, a pair of pants, and five sets of briefs. When I inquired how they had been lost, he told me that he had hung out his clothes to dry on the line outside the dormitory and had found them gone a few hours later. "Maybe they just walked away," he said with a smile on his face.

I was perplexed at the boy's reaction. There he sat with the same broad smile on his face even as he described the theft of nearly his whole wardrobe. I would have been enraged if this had happened to me. I tried to elicit a stronger reaction from him. "So, all these clothes of yours were stolen?" I asked. He simply shrugged and smiled. For the next few minutes I listed the possibilities for him: the thief could have been one of his classmates, or perhaps someone from the senior class, since there were a couple of seniors who were known to be of dubious character, or possibly a villager who had snuck up one day and helped himself to whatever he found on the clothesline. I suggested that he set a trap to find out who the thief was: he could leave a shirt or two on the line and we would watch to see who removed it. At this suggestion, the boy's eyes wandered for the first time during our

*conversation as if he were searching for a way to tell me that he
didn't want to set a trap because it would embarrass him just as
much as the thief. Even as his eyes wandered, though, the puzzling smile remained on his face the whole while.*

"Doesn't anyone ever get angry?" I used to wonder in my first
years in Micronesia. The kind of conversation recounted above would
happen frequently, as students would relate with a smile on their face,
how their last pair of underwear had been stolen or how they had suffered some other injustice. I could only marvel at their equanimity as
they joked about their misfortune. People came across as so friendly
and gentle in their behavior toward one another, some of us wondered
whether they ever experienced strong negative emotions. If they did,
how were these feelings expressed and how did these people deal with
whatever triggered their anger?

It took me years to understand that small Pacific Island societies
are much better organized to prevent conflict than to resolve it once
it occurs. Hostile parties can easily tear apart small communities, and
even small quarrels are magnified in tiny populations. Keeping the
family and community united, with its members on good terms with
one another, is an overriding concern in Micronesia, as we have seen
time and again.

One strategy for preventing conflict is to impose restraints on individualism in the community. Micronesians are trained from an early
age to conform to the expectations of the group; they learn over time
to subordinate their own personal interests to the good of the community. In this type of society the flair and creativity of the individual
may have to be sacrificed, but this compromise is seen as necessary
for maintaining harmony on the island. Quirky artistic types who are
liable to challenge the group will always represent a threat to this
harmony.

The deeply ingrained respect behavior in all Micronesian societies, already discussed in Chapter 7, is another important means of
forestalling conflict. The formal pattern of respect within a family,
with its emphasis on age and gender, may have created a hierarchical
structure among family members and some social distance between
them, but it also helped to keep the peace. The public deference that
was supposed to be paid to authorities in the village or island served

the same purpose. The type of open exchange that Americans favor in public meetings could result in hurt feelings and lingering animosities in an island society, for it is difficult to separate the issue from the person in such communities. Better to defer respectfully than to create rifts or even fault lines between people that might require years to mend.

If misunderstandings did develop between two parties despite the precautions taken to avoid such things, island societies made use of a third party to help resolve them before the matter got out of hand. One friend of mine recalled how, when he was still a boy, he was hurt by something that his father said to him in anger. He immediately left the house and stayed with an aunt, a favorite of his, for the next few days. His aunt not only sheltered him and soothed his feelings, but also spoke to his father, her brother, and settled the differences between the boy and his father. Others recall asking their uncle or some other older relative to help when problems arose between them and their parents. This was a particularly important means of dealing with young people, who could be driven to take their own lives if these bad feelings were not resolved. The same strategy was commonly used when trouble broke out in the village, as we will see later in this chapter. In such cases, the village chief or some other respected figure might be summoned to put an end to problems between one family and another, or even between one segment of the community and another. On whatever level the strategy was used, the principle was the same: call on the services of a higher authority to reconcile the two parties rather than leaving it in their own hands to do so.

If all else failed, an aggrieved party could resort to withdrawal. This was and still is a common enough response in the islands when a problem arises and a confrontation threatens. The young man who was having problems with his father took this route when he left home to live with his aunt for a time before she was able to mend the relationship after a talk with his father. Withdrawal is the same strategy that dozens of young people, most of them males, have chosen when they have decisively removed themselves from their families following quarrels or misunderstandings of one sort or another. We may refer to this as suicide, but the young person's response is viewed in the eyes of most islanders as withdrawal (of the most permanent type, of course).

A good illustration of withdrawal, although in an indirect manner, is the story of a young high school student in Yap who had been bullied by another student for several weeks. The bullying never developed into a fistfight between the two; it usually took the form of minor harassment in class, as when the older student would repeatedly poke the back of the other with a pen or whisper insulting remarks about the student. Never in the course of all this did the victim report anything to the American principal of the high school, much less tell his own family what was going on. When his patience had come to an end, the student went out one weekend and got thoroughly drunk. He was still experiencing a bad hangover when he was summoned to the principal's office on Monday morning and asked to explain his conduct. All he could tell the principal is that he was indeed drunk. Immediate action was taken against this boy who had violated school regulations: he was expelled from high school. When he returned home that day he explained to his father that the principal had thrown him out of school for drinking, even while omitting any reference to his troubles with the bully that had driven him to such action. Knowing that his father never would have accepted his son's voluntary withdrawal from school, the boy simply manipulated the situation to have his withdrawal appear to be forced on him by school authorities. He was able to utilize an old strategy, withdrawal, without taking personal responsibility for it.

Expressing Anger

The young American teacher coaching his high school baseball team in their last practice before the final game of the season was befuddled. His shortstop, one of the best players on the team, had just made a sloppy play on an easy ground ball, letting the ball hop between his legs. Then, to make matters worse, he had turned toward one of his teammates and joked about the error. In a matter of seconds, the whole team was convulsed in laughter as they all responded to his casual remarks. The coach, infuriated that his team was taking their final practice so lightly, walked onto the field and loudly lashed out at the shortstop for the error and, even more, for his lackadaisical attitude. When he finished his tongue-lashing, he told the batter to hit a few more ground balls to the shortstop.

*The shortstop resumed his position and fielded the first ball
hit to him cleanly. Biting his lip in determination—or was it a
suppressed smirk?—he rifled the ball to first base well wide of
the bag. As the ball sailed past the first baseman, the shortstop
stood there impatiently with his hands on his hips. The shortstop
had to move quickly to the right to field the next ground ball,
flipping it sidearm to first as he did. The ball flew over the head
of the first baseman. Three more ground balls, all stopped by the
shortstop, but all of the throws off the base. The coach watched
this performance from the bench with growing impatience, but
fully aware now that he was witnessing retaliation for his angry
outburst. Should he halt the practice and fire off another tirade
at his player? Should he bench him the next day and risk losing the deciding game of the season? Then he recalled what
another, more experienced teacher had once told him: "Be real
slow in declaring war on any of your students. They may not
punch you in the face, but they'll outlast you in guerrilla warfare,
island-style."*

Micronesians, like people anywhere else on the planet, become
angry at times. But thanks to their cultural predisposition to minimize conflict, their anger is usually less demonstrative and less openly
confrontational than what the American coach in this vignette might
have expected. Outbursts of rage with harsh words and threatening
gestures are very rare in the islands. This was never the Micronesian
way. Instead, anger is ordinarily concealed, or at least expressed indirectly if it cannot be masked altogether—all in the interest of sparing
oneself or others the embarrassment that public displays of anger were
sure to cause.

In view of the importance that island societies placed on keeping
up appearances, the favored strategy for dealing with anger was to
suppress it, or at least to avoid a public display of resentment. Some
years ago one of the foreign ambassadors in Micronesia hosted a
dinner party at which she had inadvertently seated two old political
rivals next to one another at the head table. Those of us who knew
the stormy history between these two men would nervously glance
over at the table to see how they were doing, but we should have
known better. Throughout the entire affair they chatted amiably with

one another, as if they were best of friends, and when they had run out of pleasantries to exchange they smiled contentedly at everyone at the table. Much the same thing happened when a former Peace Corps volunteer returned to the island on which he had lived for two years and encountered his old nemesis, a newly elected congressman from that area. As the American described it later, he and his old foe engaged in a warm two-hour conversation that belied the old animosity between them. Their deepest feelings were put on hold throughout their exchange "in a way that could only happen in Micronesia," as the American put it.

If anger must be displayed, it can always be redirected toward a safer target. This is especially true when the real object of one's anger is someone with direct authority or at least more highly positioned on the social map. Often enough this results in acting out the anger toward one's wife or children, in what western psychologists would call displacement. A Chuukese friend once told us that one of his teammates in a baseball game made a costly error that resulted in the loss of the game. The player left the field with a sheepish smile as he tried to fend off the teasing of the others on his team. As he approached his two young sons, one of whom was crying, a change of personality seemed to sweep over him. Without bothering to inquire what his son was crying about, he slapped both his boys hard across the face—one for picking on his younger brother, and the other for crying. In reality, of course, he was punishing both for his own error and the loss of the game.

One high government official, infuriated by the unreasonable demands his immediate supervisor made on him, drank himself silly every night of the week. When sufficiently drunk, he would scream into the darkness of the evening. His family rarely got a full night's sleep, but at least his wife could appear without having to hide bruises from her friends as other wives in those circumstances might have had to. Another man, when he became disturbed at a request that his father made of him, stabbed his own arm in a display of anger. At times in the islands, then, a person's anger can be deflected toward himself— an important element in the psychodynamics of suicide, which claims so many young lives each year in Micronesia.

A very common strategy used in the display of anger is passive resistance. Something akin to this is what the shortstop used after he was scolded by his coach. This served islanders well during the long years of colonial rule when one foreign administration or another would introduce some particularly obnoxious practice. People might have made an empty gesture of complying with the instructions, but they would have delayed fulfilling the obligation and excused themselves for one reason or another. Overt acceptance was followed by unrepentant foot-dragging, just as the coach's order to his shortstop to improve his fielding was followed by one wild throw after another. Whatever term might be used to describe this reaction, it is a popular form of retaliation in the islands.

A variation on this may occur when a foreigner charges into an office or store and creates a scene because he felt that he was wronged by an employee or badly served by the company. Even when the offending party lowers his eyes and apologizes meekly for the problem, the static in the atmosphere is almost palpable. As the angry customer leaves the office, eyes will shift knowingly from one employee to another and the sound of heels digging into the ground is nearly audible. Anyone who has been in the islands for long knows that the offended customer will very likely never again find satisfaction there, no matter how many assurances of help he may receive from the staff. Many outsiders have had experiences like this. Those with any sense learn to walk softly and to register any complaints they might have in a far less confrontational manner. Over the years I've learned to resist the temptation to voice my complaints openly, much less stridently; instead, I've found a touch of self-deprecating humor useful. When I had to visit a government finance department for a long overdue payment, for example, I found it helpful to reply to the inquiry on the purpose of my visit by simply saying that I was hungry. When the staff looked at me quizzically, I could explain that we had no money for lunch these days. Once the mirth abated, I was free to explain how much the overdue payment could alleviate my problem.

The most explosive displays of anger occur when a person has been drinking. Bar fights were common occurrences nearly everywhere in Micronesia during the 1960s and 1970s, the decades following the legalization of alcohol in the islands. Even today fights will sometimes break out between young drunks. Often enough people will blame alcohol for the trouble that results, but my experience is that cause and effect in such situations can often be reversed. Did the man really get angry because he was drunk, or did he get drunk because he was already angry—and needed a justification for expressing his anger? Years ago, when I was director of Xavier, a Marshallese student knocked on my door late in the evening and demanded to talk to me. He was drunk, as his red-rimmed eyes showed and as he readily admitted. He lost no time in telling me how angry he was at an implied threat I had made to the senior class that day, but he added that he could not have worked up the courage to express himself without first having a few beers. Anger drove him to drink, he implied; it was not the other way around.

The same thing happened once on Yap when a local man invited his American neighbor over to his house for a few drinks. Well into the drinking session, the Yapese voiced his anger over the way the American next door had scolded the man's son the week before when the child had wandered onto his property. To drive home the point of how angered he was at this, the Yapese man picked up a piece of wood and chased the American back to his own home. Being drunk has long served as a "free zone" for islanders, one in which they may vent their anger directly in a way that would otherwise be culturally forbidden to them. "The devil (or 'Demon Rum') made me do it," they seem to be pleading. But the truth is otherwise, as islanders and longtime expatriates know very well.

Women have their own conventions for expressing anger. They, too, have their own "free zone"—a trance state that troubled women may fall into when they are supposedly possessed by the spirit of a dead relative and begin speaking in that person's voice. Although a rare occurrence these days, "possession" permits a woman to display resentment or even outright anger toward someone in the family. Her criticism is often very direct, even scathing, but it is offered in the voice of another person, so she does not suffer the social consequences when she awakens from her trance state.

Women, who are usually less inhibited than men anyway, don't even have to resort to such means to express their negative emotions. Every so often the community is treated to the spectacle of a full-on fight between two women, usually rivals for the affection of the same man. This might happen in a store or restaurant when the two encounter one another by chance. The spectacle could consist of a heated exchange of words between the two. If the two encounter one another on the road, there is danger of a more physical contest: the two women will sometimes scream at one another, before they begin clawing and punching and trying to rip off one another's clothes.

Even among a people so culturally restrained, so hesitant to express anger publicly, the dam sometimes bursts and a fury long checked by social etiquette may erupt. The eruption, whether in the form of a shouting match or a brawl alongside the road, seems all the more threatening by contrast to the mild behavior people usually exhibit. Yet, this is the rare exception rather than the rule in Micronesia. An island people generally so respectful and good-natured should no more be judged by these incidents than Americans by the street violence that occurs in their society from time to time.

Conflict Resolution

The killing had taken place a week earlier. A group of young men were drinking alongside the road when an argument had broken out. Fueled by alcohol, the dispute quickly escalated from a loud verbal battle to a physical fight between two boys who had been on bad terms with one another since the evening began. As they grappled with one another, one of the boys threw the other to the ground, picked up a rock, and smashed it into his head. After two hard blows to the head, the boy lay motionless on the ground.

The week after that incident had been a blur of activity for the families of the two young men and anyone even distantly related to them. The funeral, which had been held the day after the death, was a time of intense emotions—far more than normal on such an occasion because of the age of the deceased and the manner in which he died. Hardly had the victim been buried and life begun to return to normal when the family of the boy who killed him started making inquiries about a formal reconciliation.

Now the stream of older people, all related to the boy who was responsible for the death, wound slowly toward the meetinghouse on the property of the victim's family. At the entrance to the meetinghouse they were met by an older man, the uncle of the dead boy, who beckoned them in. Most of the visitors carried food gifts wrapped in banana leaves or other items, which they deposited on the ground. No one spoke until the eldest of

the party, easily identifiable as the village chief, began his formal
apologies to the grieving family on behalf of the visitors.

Islanders may be generally slow to anger, but once open conflict
does break out it is not easily settled. Even when the dispute is between
two individuals, both families will almost certainly be involved. Any
serious conflict is bound to alter the relationship between the families
of both sides, so it is understandable that the families would be instru-
mental in resolving the problem.

As this vignette illustrates, it is the family of the young man who
committed the deed, not the individual himself, who is responsible for
making amends. In the formal reconciliation process, the young man
who has committed the offense will not speak; his family will speak on
his behalf. Often the family will pass off this responsibility to someone
of higher status in the community; the family may request the help of
a chief, pastor, or other respected figure to act as a spokesperson.

The procedure might vary somewhat from one place to another in
Micronesia. On some islands, instead of one of the families directly
approaching the other, both might appear before a chief to settle the
dispute. *Sakau* presented to the chief might be shared by both families on Pohnpei, while other formalities are observed in Yap. Yet, the
essential elements in a traditional reconciliation are the same throughout the region: a formal apology by the family of the offender, compensation paid to the injured family, and acceptance of the apology by
that family leading to reconciliation. The compensation offered might
be symbolized by food, as in the vignette above, but it usually included
land or money, and sometimes traditional valuables in Yap and Palau.

In some of the atolls near Yap, there is an ancient custom that any
blood shed by another must be repaid in land. Even today the offender's lineage will arrange a formal reconciliation with the other family
at which a parcel of land is turned over as compensation for the injury.
On another island, not so many years ago, the father of a young man
who had killed his wife brought several prominent friends and public
figures to the house of the young woman's family to apologize. After
the formal apology, each of the two dozen men presented the father of
the deceased woman with an envelope containing a thousand dollars.
That was simply one of the more celebrated recent examples of the
restitution that takes place at such reconciliations.

In cases like the one described in the vignette above, however, another form of compensation was sometimes added. The killer might be adopted by the victim's family in place of their dead son. For years this custom utterly baffled me. Why would people do such a thing, I wondered, unless it were to rub salt in the wounds of the killer by reminding him every day of the loss the family had suffered because of him? But wouldn't the killer's presence also serve as an irritant to the family that had suffered the loss of its young man? What purpose would be served by such an adoption? As stories of adoptions following such incidents multiplied over the years, I began to understand the logic of it all: the adopted son would serve as a replacement to the family for the labor it had lost in the death of its own son. Not only would the adopted son be obligated to provide support for the family he had injured, but the adoption would bind together the two families to ensure that they did not remain forever alienated from one another. Seen in this light, the adoption of the killer makes good sense.

Island practice toward resolving conflicts, then, differs significantly from western practice. It recognizes the need to restore peace between the two families rather than simply to exact punishment of the individual who was at fault. If a young man injures or kills someone, it is his family that will pay the price of his misdeed. In the past, before the creation of a western law enforcement system, it would have left the punishment of the wrongdoer and the control of his future behavior to his own family. His family, which had lost a valuable piece of land or other treasures, to say nothing of the shame they suffered, would have had a great stake in seeing to it that the young man did not bring further harm to his family. In essence, this system mobilized the family to exercise greater vigilance over its errant members—a strategy that is being increasingly explored even by western societies today. As in cases of wife beating and other domestic violence, the family was fully expected to be able to deal with its own problems. Finally, despite the western punishment system today, genuine peace between Micronesian families will only be satisfactorily secured after the two families have met to work out their own traditional reconciliation. Without this, bad feelings will not be assuaged, even if the offender is sentenced to a prison term.

Some forms of conflict, however, cannot be as easily resolved. Disputes over land rights can continue for decades, causing a slow simmering anger that hardens feelings even if it doesn't bring the contending parties to violence. Land, as we have already seen, is not only a precious heirloom but an extension of the collective identity. Challenging someone's claim to land by jumping boundaries or contesting property rights is bound to take on cosmic proportions. The fight gets all the nastier if the two opposing parties are closely related to one another—something that is happening ever more frequently today as the shape of the family and inheritance patterns change. Everywhere in Micronesia men are claiming as their own individual property what would have been regarded as lineage land in the past.

Land disputes seem resistant to fast settlement. There is not the same readiness to rely on a third party to handle these disputes as there is in cases of violence between families. Even the government courts established in order to resolve just such matters seem hesitant to offer judgments on land cases. Like anyone else in an island society, island judges would prefer to wiggle out of making a tough decision that they know will invariably alienate many people in their community. But the long delays, sometimes stretching on for years, can have another explanation: an instinctive island distaste for trying to resolve any problem when passions are high. Micronesian practice is to postpone a decision until after some of the emotional heat cools down, even if this may take years. In traditional times a land dispute might lie undecided for decades until one of the parties had died and it no longer was the burning issue it once had been. In such matters time may heal, but meanwhile bitterness persists and is often passed down from one generation to the next.

Handling Uncertainty and Loss

Facing Uncertainty

Rosa studied her calf for several minutes. Her right leg had suddenly become swollen just about two weeks ago and had taken on an angry red color. The appearance was worse than the pain, but still she was very nervous about the swelling. As soon as she noticed the swelling she went to the hospital to see one of the doctors. He had dismissed the problem as unimportant, giving her some mild pain medication and telling her to soak the leg three times a day. But the problem persisted.

Next she had visited an aunt of hers, an elderly woman who had a reputation as skilled in massage. She remembered, years ago, her mother sweeping her hand toward a shelf filled with different kinds of medication in a pharmacy and telling her that good massage could take care of more problems than that whole shelf full of medicine. Maybe her mother was right, but massage hadn't taken care of Rosa's swollen leg. She had been going to get her leg massaged for a week now, but there had been no improvement.

As Rosa contemplated her swollen leg, she couldn't help wondering what brought on the problem. Could it have been her bad dealings with Rieko? For months now she had been angry at her cousin Rieko for the trouble she had been causing in the family, but her feelings had become even stronger over the past few weeks. Come to think of it, her anger intensified about the time her leg problem started. Could the swollen leg be the result of stress due to the anger she was feeling? Or maybe Rieko herself was responsible for the problem. Could she have used sorcery or some kind of curse to cause the affliction? When she was growing up, Rosa had heard hundreds of stories of such things, and now and then she would still meet someone who claimed to have had sorcery used on her. Still, she wasn't sure that she believed in such things. After all, she was a Christian, wasn't she?

But you never know, she thought to herself. Some powers, for good and for bad, are beyond our understanding. Better to be safe when it comes to such things. Then she rummaged through the drawer for a medal of Our Lady of Lourdes, one that was said to have been blessed by the pope himself, and placed it on her swollen leg. She would leave it there for the rest of the day, she decided.

The future is filled with uncertainties for us all. For islanders, limited in their understanding of the workings of the natural world and subject to the powerful social forces always operating on their lives, uncertainty was everywhere. Acutely aware of their fragile control over events, Micronesians were always looking for ways to extend this control. How to guarantee a good breadfruit or taro or pandanus harvest in coming years? How to ensure a successful fishing catch that would feed the family during the days to come? How to cure a family member who was taken sick? And in the old days when interisland warfare was common, how to safeguard people in the event of an attack?

People took the precautions they could, given the knowledge they had acquired about such things. They practiced horticulture based on principles acquired through trial and error over generations. They had a supply of reliable fishing techniques and a knowledge of good fishing grounds that was accumulated over the years. They had an understanding of basic herbal medicine and massage techniques that were proven to work under certain circumstances. They had battle strategies and a defense system that offered a basic measure of security. In other words, they were equipped with whatever they could cull from their own experience and that of their ancestors to help get them through life.

Still, disasters occurred. Life was filled with unexpected threats that they could not always parry with the weapons at their disposal.

When a virulent epidemic broke out, for example, they could not turn to laboratory research to help them puzzle out the nature of the disease and devise a remedy. There was not the understanding of the basic science we take for granted today that would point them to a reasoned explanation of the epidemic and a rational understanding of how they might overcome it. Traditional Micronesians lacked the tools to do any of this, and so were slow in developing any interest in speculation. Like so many other teachers, I found early on that my island students had little interest in most of the "why" questions with which we tried to tickle their curiosity in the classroom. "Why is the sky blue?" *What difference does it make?* "Why does ice float?" *We can happily work at the math needed to determine specific density, but the question itself does not especially turn us on.*

Islanders have always opted for the personal, in keeping with the island view of reality, rather than what we would call the scientific to explain the uncertainties of life. "There is no such thing as an accident," a respected student of Micronesian life and culture once observed. When faced with a mysterious illness, islanders' thoughts would not instinctively turn to viruses or hormones or blood cells; they would turn to people. If an older person was suddenly taken sick, the family would surely ask who (not *what*) was responsible for such a misfortune. The guiding assumption was that someone was ill disposed toward the sick party and so had used his powers to bring on the illness. If that were the case, they would have to muster whatever powers they could call on to counter the spell of the angry party. Here again, as we have seen in so many other areas of island life, everything was personal.

The belief that natural forces and spiritual powers could be channeled to control events either to help or harm people was widespread. What westerners call "magic" and islanders call "medicine" provided the toolkit for doing this. A combination of herbs, charms, and potions could be used to subdue others as well as to protect against the sorcery of enemies. This belief survives even to the present day, with the charms and potions incorporating elements of Christianity as well as of the traditional religious systems.

When I was working in Chuuk some years ago, a young man whose wife had left him for another man appealed to love magic to invoke the goddess Inemes for help in winning back his wife. The formula, as he copied it down in a notebook, involved making a potion from leaves and body parts of insects while he performed ritual gestures and chanted a prayer. The whole mixture then had to be applied to the man or the woman in one another's presence. Other concoctions could be used to heal the sick once it was discovered who had cursed the sick person in the first place, or to deflect other types of evil spells. One day a boy came to me for some blessed holy water that he wanted to put into a small vial and strap to his leg while he raced in the inter-island track-and-field games. When I teased him about using church sacramentals to win the race, he was quick to point out that he was willing to depend on his own legs to win. He did not have any intention of using the amulet against any of his competitors, he assured me. The holy water was just a small defensive measure that would repel any magic that others might direct toward him during the race.

Predicting the future, like discerning the hidden causes of misfortunes, was important in maintaining control over one's life. Micronesians commonly used divination to seek answers for such questions. A practice known as *pwe*—tying knots randomly in four coconut leaf strands, counting the knots in each by fours, and converting the final numbers into the answer to a yes-or-no question—was nearly universal throughout the region. Other methods were also used. One of the most popular involved scattering pebbles or certain types of leaves on the ground and observing the pattern to find an answer to a question. Divination of this kind was used to determine the answer to both pedestrian questions (*Will tomorrow be a good day for fishing?*) as well as weightier matters (*Is such-and-such a person responsible for the misfortune that has befallen our family?*). The world was replete with sources of power that could be tapped to answer such questions, Micronesians believed, just as some westerners today resort to astrology to seek the answers in the stars.

Islanders might not practice these forms of divination any longer, but there are other ways of probing for information. Some who have become Christian open the Bible and let their finger fall on a line, which they will accept as a prophetic answer to any question they might have. As a Catholic priest, I have been approached by countless persons who press money into my hand and request that I pray for an answer to their question. Usually this is not so much a matter of looking into the future as discerning what has happened in the past. People will ask for help in finding lost items or discovering the whereabouts of missing relatives. One woman, I recall, told me that a large sum of money was missing from the small store she ran. Implicit in her request for help was the identity of the employee who made off with the money, even if the lost sum itself could not be recovered.

In a world as personal as that which Micronesians inhabited, it is hardly a surprise that they would have turned to certain people to protect them from its dangers. In the past every island and every village seemed to have its patron spirits to turn to in times of need. These patron spirits were often the spirits of ancestors reputed to have power long after their death. In some places each family had its own deceased members who would provide protection. They could be counted on to help their devotees in times of famine, sickness, conflict, and any other type of adversity.

These deities may be forgotten today, but their patronage has been invested in the Christian God who has replaced them. Islanders today who worship the God of the scriptures can appeal to this god as they might have to the deities in an earlier age. Just as islanders cling to belief in the efficacy of the personal rather than the rational in determining the course of events, they also appeal to personal intervention for protection from any damaging effects. The importance of the personal is a thread that runs through island history. Perhaps it helps explain why religion remains such a critical part of life in Micronesia, like other Pacific islands, even today. We need not discount the depth and sincerity of the personal faith of Micronesians today to understand why Christianity has been such a good fit for island life.

Loss of a Loved One

I was sitting in the Jesuit residence preparing to go down to my office when a phone call came asking for a priest to visit a local man who was close to death. I was given directions to the house, and five minutes later his wife was ushering me into the bedroom in which her husband was lying. Someone brought me a chair, but I declined and stood at the bedside for a moment taking in the scene. There were ten people in the room all standing around silently. The man seemed to be in his late seventies and had been sick for over a month, I was told. His imminent death was no surprise to anyone, given his age and his medical history. He had taken a turn for the worse just a day or two before, and now everyone in the family was preparing for the end. The family members looked tired; most had stood watch with him for the last twenty-four hours without rest. There were no tears, but the pain on the faces of all those gathered around the man's bed was clear.

As I began the prayers for the dying, the rest of the family inched a little closer to the bedside. Then I stopped, laid my hand on the head of the sick man, and asked each person in the family to come forward and do the same as we prayed silently for him. There were still no tears, but I noticed the quivering lips and the moist eyes of some of those who came to his bedside to pray over him. When one of the women returned to her place, she covered her face with a towel and silently rocked back and forth for a moment or two. I continued the prayers, anointing with oil the head and the hands of the dying man, while the family stared intently at the floor. At the end of the ritual, I blessed the man and kept my hand on his head for a few moments. Then came the first tears, as the others in the family understood that we were saying our collective farewell. I wanted to prolong that moment for the sake of the family, but they seemed to realize what was going on in my mind. One of them turned to me and said quietly, "That's OK. You can go, Father. Just leave him to us. We'll take care of him now."

Coping with the loss of a close relative or a spouse is one of the greatest challenges that islanders face. How could this not be so in a society in which personal relationships are so highly prized? The cultural features surrounding the illness and death of a relative or friend may have much in common with people grieving a loss in other parts of the world, but they can also illustrate the distinctive way in which Micronesians handle death and other kinds of personal loss.

Micronesians fear the prospect of dying away from their relatives even more than death itself. Those living abroad who are nearing the end will make every attempt to return to their family to die. When their physical condition makes this impossible, close family members will begin assembling from distant parts to be with them in their final days, no matter what the cost. It is important for the sick person to be surrounded by family members at the end. If the sick person is in a local hospital, one or two members of the family might be assigned to provide care around the clock; but as the person's condition worsens, the numbers grow. When I was visiting the hospital on pastoral visits, it was easy to gauge the condition of the patient by the number of people near the bed. If ten or fifteen people were around the bedside, with relatives spilling out of the cubicle into the corridor, it was clear that the end was near. The sick would prefer to die in their own homes in the comforting presence of their own families, of course. But if the sick person is confined to the hospital, that is where the relatives will gather.

Some of my most memorable experiences were the visits I made to dying people in hospitals or homes, visits like the one described above. Relatives would be gathered around the bedside anxiously doing the little things that might bring comfort to the sick person and straining to hear anything he might have to say. The last words of a dying person command the attention of the entire family, whether it be instructions on family inheritance, personal wishes on how the burial be conducted, or a final bit of counsel for the family. One or two of the close relatives may be mopping the brow of the dying person or gently massaging an arm, while the others sit around with their faces drawn tight in a glum expression. As the end draws closer, some of those sitting around the bed or in the corridor may stand in anticipation of the last breath. Some will weep quietly, others will simply look pained. There is usually little drama at the very end—perhaps some sobs and quiet tears, but none of the grief performance that until recently was so common at the wake or burial.

As in all cultures, islanders show the desire to cling to something of the person who has passed away. Long ago people in some places would allow the body to remain unburied until it decayed, afterward saving the bones and later burying them close to the house. Sometimes islanders would snip a lock of hair from the head of the deceased to save as a memento. Generally speaking, however, islanders do not save the personal possessions of the deceased, for there is a long tradition nearly everywhere of disposing of these as grave goods, objects that should either be burned or buried with the body.

Micronesians have always considered it a sacred duty to bury the deceased on his own island. Hence, the family will spare no expense in flying the body, accompanied by close relatives, back to his own island for burial. Other family members will take out a loan if they must to pay for their ticket to attend the interment. The specific burial site depends on local custom. In most islands a burial spot close to the residence was preferred. Today the gravesite may even be a room added to the dwelling for this purpose; or it might be a small separate enclosure close to the residence. In Palau and Yap for cultural reasons, and in the low-lying coral atolls for sanitation reasons, the burial nearly always takes place in a cemetery.

The deceased person is not only mourned by the whole family but also memorialized as part of that family. The funeral practices in Micronesia have as much to do with the surviving family as with the individual who has passed away. While tribute is paid to the departed individual, the mourners clearly recognize that with the death of one of its members, the family must gather to repair the wound that was inflicted by this loss. Thus, the death is an occasion for looking inward, reflecting on the state of the family, and taking steps for addressing

Fig. 13. Kosraean family in mourning (1978). Courtesy of Harvey Segal.

any problems that the family might have been experiencing. Nearly everywhere in Micronesia the traditional funeral customs include a formal time of reconciliation to heal any wounds within the family. At the gathering of the entire extended family, individuals will step forward to confess problems they might have had with others in the family and then ask for forgiveness from all. The death of one of its members is a privileged time for an island family, allowing members to be unusually forthright in the expression of their feelings. Many tears are shed on such occasions. The net effect is to draw the family closer together as it attempts to tighten its ranks after the loss of one of its members.

Just as the individual derived his identity from membership in the family, so his death impels the family to memorialize his loss by closing ranks within its membership. Perhaps this is the most meaningful gesture of tribute that could be paid to the dead person. The individual lives for the family, and his death consolidates the family. Beyond this, the island family clings to its hope, founded more on Christian belief today than any traditional religious system, that the family will be reunited in the afterlife and restored as it was on earth.

The Calamities of Life

Many years ago I had just arrived at an island in the western part of Chuuk to take up residence for a few months to begin learning the local language. My host was a middle-aged man from the village in which I was to be living. He greeted me at the dock, escorted me to my home, where I dropped my belongings, and promptly led me on a tour of the village.

I couldn't help but notice that many of the houses there seemed new: simple one-room homes constructed from plywood and mounted on cement blocks, with corrugated tin roofs and windows consisting of plywood panels opening outward. My host explained that a typhoon the year before had destroyed half the houses on the island. Most were dwellings built from scrap materials—whatever wood and tin could be scavenged, along with local materials—and so they were not strong enough to withstand the force of the typhoon. Afterward, the U.S. government surveyed the damage and supplied to those who had lost their homes cheap building materials for these new "typhoon houses," as they were called.

As we continued our walk through the village, he stopped and swept his hand to point out his own house. It was built on a cement foundation, perhaps dating from prewar Japanese times, but the building itself was a patchwork of what remained of the old cement walls and a jumble of scrap materials of every sort. My host apologized for the appearance of his house but explained that he was declared ineligible for the new typhoon housing that was handed out to those whose houses had been lost in the typhoon. The concrete base of the house was still usable, he was told, and so he was expected to make the other repairs on his own. This he had done, using whatever materials he could find.

My host then began explaining how proud he had been of his old home, how he had secured the services of one of the best carpenters on the island to help him put up the walls, and how he had even installed a drop ceiling to muffle the sound of rainfall on the tin roof. Suddenly the typhoon had ripped through the village and torn apart the house, he added. How sad, I thought. But my host began giggling as he described the fury of the typhoon on that fateful day, and broke into open laughter as he recounted how the pieces of roofing, one by one, were stripped by the wind, as his family huddled in a corner of the house trying to keep themselves dry. Then, as the wall panels were ripped away, his family had to charge into the face of the storm to find shelter somewhere else. As he ended his story, he was so convulsed with laughter that I had to laugh with him.

One common way that islanders deal with disappointment, even catastrophe, is to joke about it. People in Micronesia may take the loss of loved ones very seriously, and quarrels over land can continue for years, as we have seen, but damage to property and natural disasters represent a different order of misfortune altogether. So do many of the personal setbacks, such as failure in school or loss of a business, that westerners would regard as tragic.

The student who had smiled while telling his teacher of the theft of his last pair of underwear showed the same reaction as the man who had lost his home in a typhoon. What can a person do but make light of such misfortunes? What has happened has happened, and there is no way of reversing the past. Moreover, the loss of property or money or a schooling opportunity is of something that can be recouped in time. So why not laugh at it, as people would at a person who has taken a hard fall or otherwise embarrassed himself? Laughter eases the pain and the embarrassment of both the victim and the bystander.

Sometimes the humor is even expressed in song. A group of Pohnpeian women who were forced by the Japanese to labor in the rice fields even as the American counteroffensive began in World War II composed a song about their plight. The women compared themselves to frogs as they hopped around the rice paddies working from dawn to dusk, with time out only to scramble for shelter during air raids. Whatever miseries the women might have undergone at the time, they could never sing this song afterward without breaking into gales of laughter. Similar songs about World War II survive on Guam, an island that was captured by the Japanese at the outbreak of war and remained under Japanese control until it was retaken by the Americans a year before the end of the war. One of them is a satiric plea to good old Uncle Sam not to forget his family but to come back and help when they needed him. It is still played at barbeques on the island today, always mirthfully and without any hint of self-pity.

An American friend once told me that she was never so shocked as when she listened to an islander describe as a humorous event a serious medical operation that he had undergone a year or two earlier. If she had been telling the story, she said, it would have been done in solemn tones expressing how close she was to death. But the story as she heard it was a big joke: needles stuck into all parts of the body, the blinding light in the operation room, the chatter of the nurses, the lapse into unconsciousness, and even the persistent problems throughout the long period of recovery. There is no need to turn this into a morbid event, the narrator seemed to be saying, when it was just another of those past experiences that can be looked back on with humor.

The Micronesian who told her the story might have used the same disarming humor if he had been telling her about flunking out of college, losing a large sum of money in a scam, or going broke when his business failed. The house just blown away in the fury of a typhoon wind that might have killed the whole family? Bombs dropping all around us, uprooting trees and scattering earth? Forced labor long hours each day that left us exhausted and in constant fear of our lives? What can we do but laugh about it all!

Humor is sometimes also used as a way of parrying slights from other people. If someone walks into the house of another and begins to disparage its condition, the host might just take the matter one step further: "If you think the roof is in bad shape, let me tell you this story about how a floor panel once fell out and a guest tumbled to the ground." If a visitor makes a belittling remark on the culture, the person from that island might make another five or six negative observations on his own culture. Self-deprecation and the humor that accompanies it can be a shield used to deflect insults and save embarrassment, even while sparing a person from conflict.

Overall, playful humor has a large role in Micronesian life. It puts a distinctive island stamp on even the darkest of days and the most painful moments of the past—perhaps not the loss of persons or land, but the loss of just about everything else. It dispels embarrassment in uncomfortable situations, just as it can be drawn on to disarm those who would belittle one's home and one's culture. Island humor proclaims: "We laugh not at one another, but with each other." It also expresses the optimism and hope with which Micronesians generally view the future.

In Summary

A Wild Ride through a Dimly Lit Place

An encounter with a culture, especially a culture as different as those in Micronesia, is always a wild ride. I'm reminded of a theme park ride I took years ago when we were packed into a car that hurtled through one tunnel opening after another, each offering mysterious and sometimes frightening scenes, all of which we tried to absorb as the car dipped and tilted and plunged. I recall finishing the ride half wishing that I could see it all again, this time in slow motion, so that I could ponder the meaning of those tunnel scenes. It was a little too dark and the ride was too breakneck to catch it all the first time. Cultural explorations, like rides in the tunnel, always have to be done on the run and in dim light.

Ideally we would begin our encounter with a culture by seeing it through the eyes of one born there. It would be so much easier if the cultural plan were etched onto our minds and hearts, so that it made sense to us as to those who grew up in the culture. But, unfortunately, that never happens. Instead, we encounter the culture bit by puzzling bit—witnessing smiles at the oddest moments, dry eyes when we would have expected tears, harsh put-downs of those who in our judgment deserve far better, spineless reactions when a strong response seems to be called for, and on and on. The truth is that we stumble into an understanding of a culture just as an infant learns to walk and talk and make sense of the world—slowly and awkwardly.

We can read every ethnographic book in the library but we will still be surprised and often shocked by what we encounter in real life. There is no shortcut for understanding a culture. We can come to an intellectual understanding of the elements in a different culture, but to grasp a culture as a whole—to appreciate how it works and to predict accurately responses from islanders—may be the work of a lifetime. Genuine understanding of a culture can only be gained slowly and painfully on a trial-and-error course over many years, and even then the image remains fuzzy and the picture incomplete.

This book may not be able to short-circuit this process, but it might serve as a travel guide for those who will never have the opportunity to make the journey of cultural exploration for themselves. Like any travel guide, it can attempt to list the most remarkable features of the country, offer directions on how to reach them, and warn against tourist traps that misrepresent the wonders of the place. It can also caution visitors to avoid misunderstanding the customs of the local residents. All this I have tried to do in this little cultural guidebook on island life.

If nothing else, this book may prevent newcomers from making blinkered judgments about some of the more puzzling and dubious features of island cultures. Why do island men treat their wives and sisters so badly? Why are islanders so withholding of what should be public information? What's the point of wasting all that food at a village feast? If we can see the culture as a system with a logic of its own rather than merely a pastiche of exotic customs, there is a good chance that we might be more sympathetic to these puzzling features. At least we will understand that they are outgrowths of a cultural system that has an internal logic. That alone might make us a bit less ready to fly to the attack when we confront what we regard as an "abuse." If it causes us to hesitate a bit and check our own assumptions before making harsh and unwarranted judgments, this book will have served its purpose.

Peaks in the Micronesian Landscape

There is, as I have insisted from the outset, a logic to island culture. Throughout the chapters of this book I have presented several themes and attempted to lay out my own understanding of the way in which islanders think about each subject. Along the way I have highlighted some of the differences from conventional western thinking.

Here, without attempting to review everything covered in the previous chapters, I will try to draw a brief outline of what we might call the peaks in the cultural landscape. They represent what could be seen as the most prominent cultural features in island society, those value clusters that are foundational for Micronesia. They don't cover everything, but are broad enough to offer the beginnings of a summary. The features are three: personalization, group identity, and collaboration. They represent cultural features that are important in any society, but they are especially helpful in distinguishing the landscape in a Micronesian culture.

The Personal Face

People worldwide, no matter what their cultural background, would like to think that they value personal interactions with individuals. And so they do—with family and close friends, and perhaps to some extent with passing acquaintances. But in small island societies, in which nearly everyone falls into one of these categories, personalization fashions the rules of behavior toward everyone, not just toward a small segment of the population. The universal person-to-person quality of social interaction charms outsiders, who find this characteristic of island life so endearing, but it also has consequences that westerners often find less attractive.

Island people respond to persons, according to their relationship, age, and status, with different degrees of respect. But respect is not something that can be readily switched on and off. A close relative or a highly regarded person will retain those personal features and be treated accordingly whether he shows up in a customs line at an airport, in a roomful of applicants for a job, or in the court docket. Because it is so difficult to strip the individual of his personal features, the evenhanded treatment and equity that have so central a place in western ideologies represent an ideal beyond the grasp of most islanders. Preferential treatment is built into the social framework of island life. Hence, bureaucratic efficiency is compromised in a society in which there is no such thing as the faceless "public."

Concern for personal feelings is developed to an art form in the islands, as we have seen. A respect for the plain truth, so revered in western thinking, yields to a situational approach in which a personal response is shaped according to the needs of the person with whom one is speaking. In the effort to avoid hurting someone's feelings, what westerners might call "truth" is often fudged. The crafted response almost always wins out over the objective description of things as they are.

Social circumspection is bound to be a key element in any interaction to avoid the risk of giving offense. Keeping the peace and the goodwill of others in the community is critical in island culture. Confrontations, even minor ones, can have major consequences in small societies. Thus, the patterns of behavior in all dimensions of island life are organized in such a way as to minimize the danger of conflict. The emphasis on respect in all its forms serves this purpose. The ambivalence with which islanders speak out of consideration for their listeners, the marks of deference that respect behavior demands, the long pauses in conversation to provide openings for others to interject their opinions—all these serve that purpose. This can slow interaction and make it burdensome to carry on a conversation, but it also guards against running roughshod over another person in a social situation.

The personal dimension in life is carried over even into areas that startle westerners. Illness, for instance, was frequently attributed to sorcery worked by someone who had a grudge against the sick party. For islanders everything had a personal face—the elements of the physical world as well as social interaction.

The Primacy of Group Identity

Micronesian cultures have always emphasized the group over the individual, the "we" over the "I." The family, or kin group, is not so much the springboard from which a person is launched to build his own life as an anchor for the individual. The kin group bestows an identity, a sense of personal worth, a refuge in which a person can find a loving home no matter how badly he has failed in his life. All this justifies the primacy of the kin group over the individual in the eyes of traditional Micronesians.

The family not only gave the individual an identity, but also provided access to land and other resources. After all, land was corporately owned nearly everywhere in Micronesia. The individual also could depend on the family for protection and security.

Because of the importance of the kin group, the individual did not have the option of walking away from the family, even from what westerners would call a dysfunctional family. Where westerners might say, "Be true to yourself," islanders would render the saying as "Be true to your family." Clearly, individual self-reliance never had the same value for islanders that it had for Americans.

The implications of all this for the individual are important. The person might be obliged to sacrifice his educational future, the wealth that he might have accumulated, and even the choice of his marriage partner for the good of the family. In the islands the good of the kin group always takes precedence over the good of the individual. Under such conditions, it is virtually impossible for a young man or woman to leave his family to follow his own star.

Areas of Collaboration

The vital significance of group identity in island life suggests the importance of regular cooperation, even if the ways in which the group works together often pose a surprise to westerners. Collaboration is required anywhere in the world, of course, but its forms in the islands may take strange shapes.

The strict division of labor by gender, with certain tasks assigned to males and others to females, is one that westerners find most challenging, even though a similar division was to be found throughout the western world not too many decades ago. This hard-and-fast division of labor until recently denied women in Micronesia access to a wide range of occupational careers. Moreover, even social roles have been constrained: females have been accustomed to relying on males for protection, while males have always looked to females for peacemaking.

Collaboration of larger family groups in using landholdings to furnish food has been common everywhere in the islands. Everyone in the kin group could count on having access to the land they needed, just as they can count on receiving money or financial help from their family today. Because the land was jointly owned, however, it was difficult to secure permission to sell it, lease it, or use it for other money-making purposes.

Collaboration among members of a kin group, however, goes beyond sharing land. It includes the sharing of children within the group, as when children are adopted out to assist other members of one's broad kin group.

Fig. 14. A different view of the world (1973). Courtesy of Carlos Viti.

Clash of Worldviews

The Micronesian worldview repeatedly clashes with that of the western world, as I have noted throughout this book. These clashes are not just speculative matters, differences of approach to day-to-day life that can be shrugged off as interesting but unimportant. The clashes touch those areas in which island society is being encouraged to modernize—to get with the program, as it were. They touch on issues such as a free press, good governance, law enforcement, gender equality, and economic development. The main clashes of worldview are summarized below.

- Personal responsibility, emphasized so strongly in the West, clearly challenges the traditional emphasis in Micronesia on the primacy of the kin group. This touches many different areas: personal finances, legal responsibility and punishment for law breaking, and political forms such as the vote.
- The concept of individual rights clashes with a traditional Micronesian understanding of social order. Islanders have

always underscored what is owed others rather than what others owe them. In addition, this rights concept exaggerates the importance of the individual while downplaying the group.

- The notion of equity, equal treatment for all, that is so prized in the West is at odds with the special regard that islanders owe their own kin group and others with high status in the community.

- Western feminism that insists on direct power to women conflicts with the time-honored island practice of having women's influence mediated through men. In the eyes of westerners who call for freeing women from their shackles to men, the indirect authority of women seems belittling.

- Open sharing of information may be called for to keep the public informed, but it is tricky business in the islands because information can be used to harm individuals. Moreover, information is often withheld because of the inherent value it has and the prestige it can confer on the one possessing it.

- The expression of personal opinion that is thought to be so essential for democracy is often seen by islanders as dangerously close to the very type of open confrontation that they have been taught to avoid. Micronesians are trained to express themselves indirectly and with circumspection.

- Land, which westerners regard as a commodity, should be made available to investors willing to establish a business that can contribute to economic growth. Micronesians, however, see land as an extension of themselves rather than an item that can be traded freely.

- Western-trained economists encourage islanders to lay away some of their cash income to provide for their unanticipated needs in the future. Instead, Micronesians are inclined to invest in their kin group. They do this by providing whatever money they can to relatives in need, trusting as they do that these relatives will provide for them when they themselves require help.

As Micronesian and western approaches collide, some of the new values and conceptual apparatus from outside are gradually being embraced by islanders. Micronesians today, for example, are beginning to accept the concept of human rights and are showing an interest in using such a conceptual scheme for their own benefit. The notion of personal responsibility has also been adopted to some extent, especially in the court systems throughout the islands. Still more changes will occur as island cultures are forced to make further accommodation to modernization.

Cultural change is inevitable for all peoples, whether they might be termed "traditional" or "modern." The ongoing exchange between Micronesian island cultures and the West guarantees that further changes will be made in the mind-set and values of island peoples. This is never a painless process, of course, but it need not be made more difficult than it has to be. An understanding by westerners of the way in which islanders look at life, some comprehension of the cultural logic with which they work, could make the transition much more comfortable. That, in the end, is the purpose of this book.

SUGGESTED READING

Exploring Themes in the Chapters

CHAPTER 1

The treatment of bureaucracy in the second section of this chapter was adapted from my article "Why Our Government Offices Don't Work," *Micronesian Counselor* 22 (May 1998). This and other issues of *Micronesian Counselor* can be found on the Micronesian Seminar website: www.micsem.org.

CHAPTER 2

Kinship terms such as "lineage" and "clan" can be formidable for anyone who has not had formal training in anthropology. For a brief and simple summary of the forms the family took in the main island groups in Micronesia, you might wish to try my presentation in *The New Shape of Old Island Cultures* (Honolulu: University of Hawai'i Press, 2001), 8–12. The book goes on to discuss briefly the ways in which the family changed and the reasons for these changes. For those who want to venture further, I would suggest the much fuller and more technical treatment offered by Mac Marshall in "'Partial Connections'?: Kinship and Social Organization in Micronesia," a chapter in *American Anthropology in Micronesia: An Assessment*, edited by Robert Kiste and Mac Marshall (Honolulu: University of Hawai'i Press, 1999), 107–143. For a readable overview of the topic, you might try Roger Keesing, *Kin Groups and Social Structure* (New York: Holt, Rinehart and Winston, 1975).

Suicide is a problem that has bedeviled the islands for the past forty years. For more on the subject see Hezel, "Truk Suicide Epidemic and Social Change," *Human Organization* 46, no. 4 (1987): 283–291; Hezel, "Suicide and the Micronesian Family," *Contemporary Pacific* 1, no. 1 (1989): 43–74; and Donald Rubinstein, "Epidemic Suicide Among Micronesian Adolescents," *Social Science Medicine* 17, no. 10 (1983): 657–665. These works document the high rate among youth, especially among young males, and attempt to offer explanations for the frequency of suicide in the islands since the 1970s.

Land tenure and inheritance is another of those cultural labyrinths in which an outsider can get hopelessly lost. For this reason, those who want to push on into this field would do well to take small steps forward. You might begin with the chapter on land in my book, *The New Shape of Old Island Cultures*, 33–45.

CHAPTER 3

For an extended discussion of the growth of individualism in the islands, see my article "The Cult of the Individual," *Micronesian Counselor* 65 (January 2007). Like other issues of this publication, it can be found on the MicSem website: www.micsem.org.

Traditional chiefly authority is treated in "A Hibiscus in the Wind: The Chief and His People," *Micronesian Counselor* 20 (December 1997). For a more extended treatment of the subject, you might refer to my earlier work *The New Shape of Old Island Cultures*, 121–126. Those who are especially interested in the topic would do well to consult Geoffrey White and Lamont Lindstrom, *Chiefs Today: Traditional Pacific Leadership and the Postcolonial State* (Stanford, CA: Stanford University Press, 1997).

The introduction of the ballot and its effects on Micronesian island society is treated in my article "Island Politics," *Micronesian Counselor* 67 (May 2007).

The disconnect between human rights theory and Pacific Island thinking is a problem that has yet to be seriously addressed, in my opinion. I've tried to take up this issue in the article "In Search of a Talking Point on Human Rights," *Humanidat* 3, no. 1 (1995): 111–116. The article can be found on the MicSem website.

CHAPTER 4

One of the clearest examples of social capital in the islands I've come across is presented in the article by Glenn Petersen, "Redistribution in a Micronesian Commercial Economy," *Oceania* 57 (1986): 83–98.

For those interested in more on the impact of the cash economy on island culture, you might start with my article "The Cultural Revolution of the 60's," *Micronesian Counselor* 73 (September 2008). The spread of the cash economy, moreover, is the central theme in *The New Shape of Old Island Cultures*.

CHAPTER 5

The island understanding of how information is to be shared as well as the conflicts that arise between this understanding and the access to public information is explored in my article "Peeking into the Public Process," *Micronesian Counselor* 54 (January 2005). On the MicSem website is also a summary of a public discussion on the same topic under the title "Freedom of Information: Who Has a Right to What?" (MicSem Monthly Discussion Topic #14, May 17, 1995).

CHAPTER 6

Much of this chapter is an expansion of my article "A Teacher's Tale," *Micronesian Counselor* 78 (November 2009). This article, incidentally, was the starting point for the development of this entire book.

CHAPTER 7

Respect behavior, within the family and outside it, is taken up in slightly more detail in my book *The New Shape of Old Island Cultures* (check the index for specific references).

Those who wish to learn more about traditional chiefly authority in the islands are referred to the same sources as mentioned under Chapter 3: Hezel, "Hibiscus in the Wind: The Micronesian Chief and His People," and Hezel, *The New Shape of Old Island Cultures*, 121–126.

CHAPTER 8

This entire chapter has been excerpted and reshaped from *The New Shape of Old Island Cultures*, 108–120. The notes for that chapter can serve to direct interested readers to further references in the anthropological literature.

CHAPTER 9

This chapter, too, is drawn in great part from *The New Shape of Old Island Cultures*, 46–65. Distinctions of work along gender lines, power and protection of women, and recent changes are all discussed in greater detail there.

CHAPTER 10

There is surprisingly little in the literature on the expression of love in the islands apart from a few scattered references in the standard anthropological texts. Here I can only refer you my article "A Teacher's Tale."

CHAPTER 11

Much of the first section, "Avoiding Clashes," is drawn from my article "A Teacher's Tale."

For a fuller treatment of the role of alcohol in the expression of negative feelings, see my article "Youth Drinking in Micronesia," *Micronesian Counselor* 6 (March 1992). A fuller treatment of this topic, although limited to Chuuk, can be found in Mac Marshall, *Weekend Warriors: Alcohol in a Micronesian Culture* (Palo Alto, CA: Mayfield Publishing Co., 1979).

Women's resort to self-expression of anger and other negative feelings through a trance state is explored in my article "Spirit Possession in Chuuk," *Micronesian Counselor* 11 (July 1993). This interesting subject is dealt with in greater detail in an article I once wrote with Jay Dobbin, "Possession and Trance in Chuuk," *Isla* 3, no. 1, (1995): 73–104. This, too, can be found on the MicSem website.

Conflict resolution in the islands is taken up in my article "The Rule of Law," *Micronesian Counselor* 38 (December 2001). If you want a much fuller treatment of the issue throughout the Pacific, try this book: Karen Watson-Gegeo and Geoffrey White, *Disentangling: Conflict Discourse in Pacific Societies* (Stanford, CA: Stanford University Press, 1990).

CHAPTER 12

For a fuller description of divination and traditional religious practices in Micronesia, see Jay Dobbin, *Summoning the Powers Beyond* (Honolulu: University of Hawai'i Press, 2011).

Island practices related to death are briefly treated in *The New Shape of Old Island Cultures*, 91–94.

General Reading on Micronesia

Alkire, William. *Introduction to the Peoples and Cultures of Micronesia*. San Francisco: Cummings Publishing Company, 1977.

Ashby, Gene. *Never and Always: Micronesian Legends, Fables and Folklore*. Eugene, OR: Rainy Day Press, 1989.

———. *Some Things of Value: Micronesian Customs as Seen by Micronesians*. Eugene, OR: Rainy Day Press, 1983.

Barclay, Robert. *Melal: A Novel of the Pacific*. Honolulu: University of Hawai'i Press, 2002.

Hezel, Francis X. *The New Shape of Old Island Cultures: A Half Century of Social Change in Micronesia*. Honolulu: University of Hawai'i Press, 2001.

———. *Strangers in Their Own Land: A Century of Colonial Rule in the Caroline and Marshall Islands*. Honolulu: University of Hawai'i Press, 1995.

Kluge, P. F. *The Edge of Paradise: America in Micronesia*. New York: Random House, 1991.

Lessa, William. *Ulithi: A Micronesian Design for Living*. New York: Holt, Rinehart and Winston, 1966.

Ward, Martha C. *Nest in the Wind: Adventures in Anthropology on a Tropical Island*. Prospect Heights, IL: Waveland Press, 1989.

INDEX

wealth, 49–61, 63, 72–73, 109; accumulation of, 52–56, 58–59
Weber, Max, 20
western goods, 5, 58
women, 26, 43, 82, 102–104,
107–109, 111, 113–126, 133–137,
147–148, 179; authority of,
116–117, 121–126, 170; protection
of, 43, 102–104; work of, 8–10,
117–122, 168

Xavier High School, 14–15, 39, 76,
85, 102, 106, 121, 140, 147

yams, 8, 52, 92
Yaoch, Felix, 50
Yap, 1, 5, 8–10, 25, 28, 34, 43, 51–52,
109, 119, 124, 131, 138, 143, 147,
149, 159

zero-balance budget, 60–61

About the Author

FRANCIS X. HEZEL is a Jesuit priest who has lived and worked in Micronesia for forty-five years. At different times he has served as high school teacher, school administrator, fill-in pastor, and regional superior. He also founded and directed the Micronesian Seminar, a church-sponsored research institute that has engaged in a broad public education program for the islands. Besides conducting political education programs, workshops, and conferences on a range of concerns, he has authored over a hundred articles and produced more than seventy television programs that have been broadcast throughout the region. Over the years he has also conducted ongoing research on suicide, trance and spirit possession, mental illness, alcohol and drug use, and emigration to the United States. The author has spoken widely about social change and its impact on island societies, among many other topics. He has also written several books on Micronesian history and culture, including *The First Taint of Civilization, Strangers in Their Own Land,* and *The New Shape of Old Island Cultures.* His articles, videos, and the other products of Micronesian Seminar can be viewed online at the Micronesian Seminar website (www.micsem.org).

Production Notes for
HEZEL / MAKING SENSE OF MICRONESIA

Jacket design by Julie Matsuo-Chun.

Interior design and composition by Josie Herr
with text Sabon and display in Papyrus.

Printing and binding by Sheridan Books, Inc.

Printed on 55 lb. House White Hi-Bulk D37, 360 ppi.